Diane Turner holds an MA in Communication from Penn State University, where she taught Speech Communication, as well as Leadership and Organizational Management for eight years. For two years she was on-air consumer reporter for KDKA-TV's Evening Magazine, and she also hosted an interview show on WPSX-TV. Her recent work and research focuses on teambuilding to develop fail-safe systems for maximum quality and productivity in business and industry. Other areas of her expertise include personality analysis, conflict resolution and development of corporate communication networks. She also develops marketing and fundraising strategies for the arts, PBS, major league sports teams and other organizations and corporations.

Thelma Greco holds an MEd specializing in teambuilding from Penn State University where she was on the staff for ten years. She conducts leadership training and works with companies to develop strategic plans, assess effectiveness, build teams, manage downsizing and modify corporate cultures through her McNellis advanced story-board training. In addition to being an avid reader, she is a professional handwriting expert and a Forensic Document Examiner. Her approach to consulting is collaborative with an emphasis on the implementation phase of the change process. Her recent work also involves designing and coordinating gifted programs and teams for junior and senior high school students.

Diane and Thelma founded Quality Teambuilding Programs (QTP) in 1991. Their original teambuilding model, *The Personality Compass*, forms the basis for their Interactive Training Workshops. Clients include *Gannett News* and *USA Today* Corporate Headquarters in Washington DC, the Center for Executive Education, Trotter Corporation, Manufacturing Assistance Center (MAC) and many others. For their ground-breaking research and contributions in teambuilding and communication, based on *The Personality Compass*, the authors were selected into the 1997 National Registry of *Who's Who*. Both are married and reside with their families in Western Pennsylvania.

You may write to the authors at PO Box 206, Sarver, PA 16055, USA or fax to 001 412 353 1490. E-mail, qtp@personalitycompass.com. Web site, http://www.personalitycompass.com.

The
Personality
Compass

A New Way to Understand People

Diane Turner and Thelma Greco

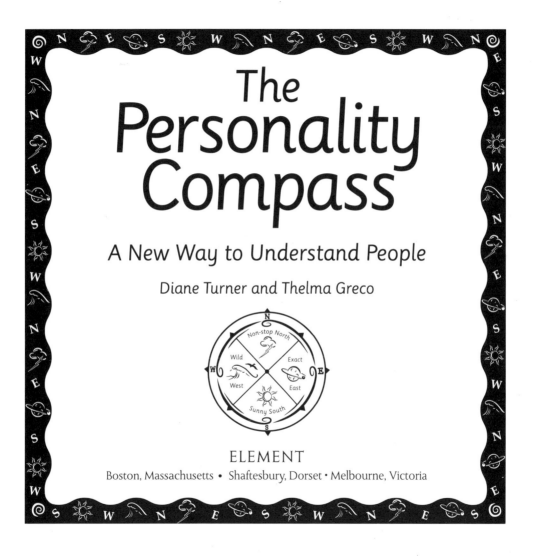

ELEMENT
Boston, Massachusetts • Shaftesbury, Dorset • Melbourne, Victoria

© Element Books Limited 1998
Text © Diane Turner and Thelma Greco 1998

First published in the USA in 1998 by
Element Books, Inc.
160 North Washington Street, Boston, MA 02114

Published in Great Britain in 1998 by
Element Books Limited
Shaftesbury, Dorset SP7 8BP

Published in Australia in 1998 by
Element Books Limited
and distributed by Penguin Australia Limited
487 Maroondah Highway, Ringwood, Victoria 3134

Illustrations by Deborah Drummond
Cover design by Max Fairbrother
Design by Mark Slader
Typesetting by Mark Slader
Printed in Hong Kong through Worldprint

British Library Cataloguing in Publication Data available

Library of Congress Cataloging in Publication Data available

ISBN 1-86204-285-3

Contents

Chapter Four Valuing the Nature of EAST

Chapter Five Valuing the Nature of SOUTH

Chapter Six Valuing the Nature of WEST

Chapter Seven People Aren't Difficult . . . Just Different

Introduction

All world travelers will have experienced visible cultural differences on visiting, say, Norway, Japan, Jamaica or the United States. The terrain and climate are different, and the people look, sound, move and behave differently. We can even feel the differences in telephone conversations we have with people from different parts of the world – from the fast-paced North to the laid-back South, and from the formal East to the casual West. Using what is already understood in a kind of universal consciousness about cultural characteristics, we have written *The Personality Compass* as a new way to understand people according to personality type. The book is a unique resource for implementing the oldest and the newest personality research to impact our lives in a positive way.

What makes *The Personality Compass* different from the myriad other books written about why people are the way they are?

- The graphic handbook format is practical and interesting to read, and is useful as a handy desktop reference.

- The familiar cultural analogy introduced through *The Personality Compass*, a unique resource for identifying personality type, is easy to comprehend, remember and use immediately to understand people.

● The premise that there are four basically different nature and personality types is supported by ancient theories, as well as by recent scientific studies.

The purpose of this book is threefold: (1) to help you to know and value yourself, (2) to help you get along better with all kinds of people and enjoy successful relationships and (3) to help you choose the right job or career to ensure the greatest degree of personal satisfaction and professional success. The goal is to provide a quick, easy and accurate way to identify your own and other people's inherent nature in order to understand the specific needs, likes and dislikes, natural talents, skills and behaviors of the four fundamental types. Understanding a person's particular nature and personality is also the key to motivating and communicating effectively with that person.

Using a universal analogy, there is a parallel between the north, east, south and west directions on a compass, the cultural characteristics of each of the four regions, and the four fundamental natures of man. For example, *The Personality Compass* refers to individuals with the typical assertive, independent and fast-paced characteristics of peoples of Northern cultures, with their strength and seafaring heritage, like that of the Scandinavians, as having a NORTH nature. Think of the determined Vikings and their powerful conquests.

Individuals who have the typical structured, conservative and reserved characteristics of peoples of the East cultures, with their formal, ritualistic heritage like that of Asians, are referred to as having an EAST nature. Think of the polite Japanese and their respect for etiquette.

SOUTH-natured individuals exhibit the typical friendly, hospitable and slow-paced characteristics of peoples in Southern cultures, such as the easy going and relaxed tropical Islanders. Think of the gregarious Jamaicans and their willingness to be helpful.

The typical adventurous, visionary, innovative characteristics of peoples of Western cultures, with their free-spirited, pioneering heritage, such as that of the North Americans, are possessed by people with a WEST nature. Think of the risk-taking Americans and their unconventional ideas.

Chapter One provides historic precedence and recent scientific evidence that supports the four major groupings of traits that distinguish the four different human natures. Chapter Two explains the cultural analogy and presents diagrams of the Personality Compass, the four different cultural clusters, at a glance, and it provides type-identification exercises and a quick test for easy use and quick identification of each nature. Each of Chapters Three through Six represents one of the four cultural natures on the Personality Compass, and provides: (1) enlightening and useful information about the qualities and talents of each and (2) graphically illustrated strategies for getting along and dealing effectively with each of the four natures. Chapter Seven reveals how inherent differences in type can create natural difficulties between people, how to minimize potential conflicts, and how to develop all four of the personality directions to ensure the highest degree of personal and professional success.

Just as symbols have been developed globally to simplify communication without language barriers, our universal terms and symbols can unify the way people from all cultures perceive and understand each other. In some way, the message clearly comes through that, just as north, east, south and west directions are equally important and without preconceived hierarchies in value, so it is with human nature. All directions, cultures and personality types are significant and integral to the whole. Knowing that can improve self-esteem and pioneer a path for peace among families, communities, and even nations. *The Personality Compass* simplifies this understanding as well as the communication process.

Chapter One

Reviewing the Four Natures of Man

Building on Classic Theories

*T*he *Personality Compass* is based on the premise that there are four clusters of human characteristics that distinguish each of the four basic natures of man as inherently different, but equally valuable in its own way. This concept is not new, but using a cultural analogy to make the information easier to remember and use is unique. History supports the divisions of human nature and personality into four fundamental groups. As early as the 5th century BC, Hippocrates, "the father of medicine", linked what he called the four temperaments to body fluids (humors), and he described similar groupings of characteristics found today in brain and biochemical studies.

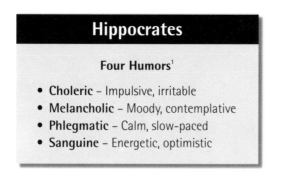

Hippocrates

Four Humors[1]

- **Choleric** – Impulsive, irritable
- **Melancholic** – Moody, contemplative
- **Phlegmatic** – Calm, slow-paced
- **Sanguine** – Energetic, optimistic

Aristotle

"Ratio of Opposites": Forces of Nature[2]

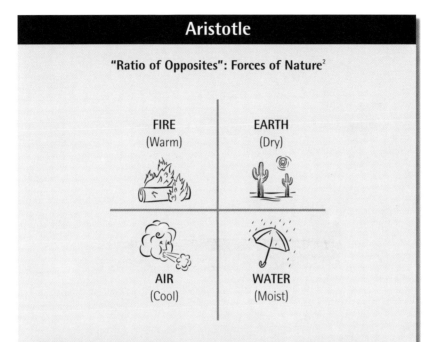

FIRE
(Warm)

EARTH
(Dry)

AIR
(Cool)

WATER
(Moist)

The Greeks viewed everything in nature as having the innate properties found within these four fundamental components of all life forces. Aristotle, in the 4th century BC, recognized a "ratio of opposites" in the distinctive properties of Fire, Earth, Water and Air in nature, which were associated with human nature and personality as well (Hardie, 1968).

Jung

The Four Basic "Functions" of Psychological Man[3]

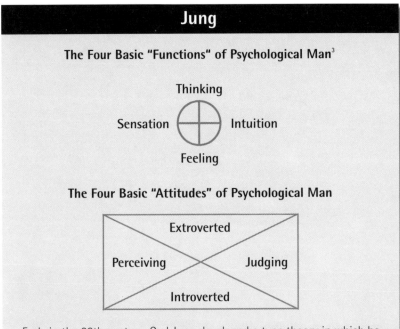

Thinking

Sensation   Intuition

Feeling

The Four Basic "Attitudes" of Psychological Man

Extroverted

Perceiving   Judging

Introverted

Early in the 20th century, Carl Jung developed a type theory in which he identified what he called the four basic functions and the four basic attitudes of man's innate nature. His research revealed that every individual has a dominant function and attitude in his personality at birth, or by very early childhood, that determines how he approaches the external world.

Myers/Briggs

The Four Basic Clusters of Personality Types[4]

Code

T = Thinking   E = Extroverted

N = Intuition   J = Judging

F = Feeling   I = Introverted

S = Sensation   P = Perceiving

Types

1 ISTJ, ISFJ, ISTP, ISFP

2 INFJ, INTJ, INFP, INTP

3 ESTJ, ESFJ, ESTP, ESF

4 ENFJ, ENTJ, ENFP, ENTP

The Myers-Briggs Type Indicator (MBTI) is based on Jungian typology and is used extensively today to test for individual personality types and the inherent interests and aptitudes of each. According to Jung, the dominant function and attitude of a person are those that are favored unconsciously over the others by an individual. Eventually, they become well developed at a conscious level as well.[5] The MBTI matches Jung's four basic functions and attitudes in different combinations. The final result is four clusters of personality types.

Watson/Crick

Deoxyribonucleic Acid [6]

In the early 1950s, JD Watson and FHC Crick discovered that deoxyribonucleic acid (DNA) carries genetic information. This discovery came as a surprise because it had previously been believed that only proteins contained enough complexity to carry inherited information. At first geneticists had great difficulty in accepting DNA as the substance of genes because of the simplicity of its chemistry – consisting of only four nucleotides linked in a long string of repeating units to form a double helix. This four-base DNA structure provides an explanation for all heredity.

Four Nucleotides That Form the Double Helix of DNA [6]

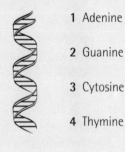

1 Adenine

2 Guanine

3 Cytosine

4 Thymine

Nomi / Besher

Blood Types[7]

Blood Type O

Queen Elizabeth and Ronald Reagan
• Goal-oriented • Strong leader • Realistic

Blood Type B	Blood Type A
Tom Selleck and Mia Farrow	Alan Alda and Jimmy Carter
• Flexible • Unconventional	• Detail-oriented • Industrious
• Creative	• Careful

Blood Type AB

John F Kennedy and Edgar Allen Poe
• Diplomatic • Harmonious • Everybody's friend

As bizarre as it may seem, a relationship between blood type and personality traits, or nature, was found by Toshitaka Nomi, with help from Alexander Besher. The breakdown of traits for people with each of the four blood types cluster in similar groupings to those of the four nature types. It is important to note, however, that no matter to what extent an individual's nature might be genetically predisposed, the billions of DNA combinations required for every human trait still result in an enormous degree of individuality within each of the four basic natures.

Friedman/Sperry

Type A/Type B[8] and Left Brain/Right Brain Discoveries

Biochemical differences have been found in what Dr Meyer Friedman refers to as Type A and Type B people. In stress and alarm reaction studies of the Type A (high stress) and Type B (low stress) personalities or natures, he discovered differences in body chemistry between the two. Specifically, the easily agitated Type A subjects produced elevated levels of epinephrine and cortisol, and the blood flow to the muscles was three times greater in Type As than in Type Bs.[9]

Dr Roger Sperry, who received the 1981 Nobel Prize in Medicine for his split-brain experiments, discovered fundamental differences in the kinds of thinking that take place in the right hemisphere of the brain (nonverbal, creative) versus that which takes place in the left (verbal, analytical). He found that brains are different at birth, with different neural circuitry which results in different cognitive processing and different potentialities among individuals. His findings indicated that it is the brain that determines one's nature, as well as one's potentiality to become a poet, a musician, an artist, a mechanic or a scientist.[10]

Type A/Type B and Left Brain/Right Brain Traits

Scientific studies by Friedman, Sperry and others provide strong evidence that our body's biochemistry has an enormous impact on who we are, how we behave and our natural strengths and weaknesses. A number of studies by contemporary neuroscientists have discovered that behavioral differences have distinctive physical expressions in the brain.[11]

Type A Temperament[12]

Assertive
Competitive
Ambitious
Fast-paced
Impatient
Hard-driving
Emphatic

Right-Brain Thinking

Rhythm
Music
Images
Imagination
Daydreaming
Color
Dimension

Left-Brain Thinking

Language
Logic
Number
Sequence
Linearity
Analysis
Calculation

Type B Temperament

Calm
Easy-going
Patient
Kind
Slow-paced
Quiet
Passive

(Note: When facing us, a person's left and right brain hemispheres appear reversed.)

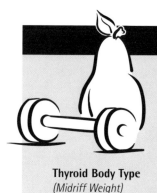

Abravanel/King

Body Types[13]

Pituitary Body Type
(Distributed Weight)
- Opinionated
- Self-confident
- Potent

Thyroid Body Type
(Midriff Weight)
- Energetic
- Witty
- Many-faceted

Adrenal Body Type
(Stomach Weight)
- Persistent
- Capable
- Focused

Gonadal Body Type
(Bottom Weight)
- Nurturing
- Helpful
- Magnetic

Elliott D Abravanel, MD, and Elizabeth A King found a link between body type and personality characteristics. They discovered ways to identify each type not only by personality traits, but by appearance and appetite. Then they designed a health, exercise and weight maintenance program for each type individually. Their work provides additional evidence that there is a strong relationship between the body's physiology and personality type.

Facial Types[14]

Square-Shaped Types
- Aggressive
- Goal-directed
- Project-absorbed
- Competitive

Oblong Types
- Spontaneous
- Enthusiastic
- Far-sighted
- Calm

Triangular Types
- Intellectual
- Judgmental
- Supersensitive
- Solitary

Round Types
- Easygoing
- Comfort-loving
- Gregarious
- Diplomatic

Physiognomy is a Chinese art that reveals an individual's personality by the study of his face. According to studies by TT Mar and others, the face is the most information-rich part of the body, and is the part we pay most attention to when communicating. Here we consider the four facial shapes and what research shows they reveal about a person's personality.

Mendel

Handwriting Types[15]

Angular Writing Style

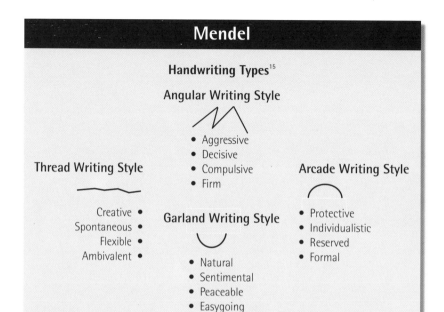

- Aggressive
- Decisive
- Compulsive
- Firm

Thread Writing Style

Creative •
Spontaneous •
Flexible •
Ambivalent •

Garland Writing Style

- Natural
- Sentimental
- Peaceable
- Easygoing

Arcade Writing Style

- Protective
- Individualistic
- Reserved
- Formal

Handwriting, which originates in the brain, reveals a person's capacity for thinking and feeling through the rhythmic harmony of the script, and involves connecting thoughts with one another. As soon as we know how a person connects his thoughts, we know his way of thinking. Many handwriting experts, including Alfred Mendel, recognize the following four writing connections which reflect the mental processes at work and the personality qualities each exhibits.

Canine Types[16]

- Excitatory – Pugnacious, passionate
- Inhibitory – Melancholy, expects nothing
- Steadfast – Quiet, self-contained
- Energetic – Productive, easily bored

Studies of temperament in animals, and dogs specifically, have revealed similar groupings of characteristics to those of human nature and personality. The most famous research with dogs is probably that of IP Pavlov in the mid-20th century. More recently, research by psychologist, David Lykken, has yielded similar results to those of Pavlov regarding the similarities of temperament in dogs and man.

Questions & Answers About the Four Personality Types

Carl Jung found through scientific research that personality types exist, whether or not people deny their existence.[17]

Question How can billions of people fall into only four basic nature or personality groupings?

Answer *The same way that billions of people fall into only three or four races: Negroid, Mongolian or Caucasian (some consider Indian as a fourth race, while others include Indian as part of the Mongolian race).*

Question How do you account for the uniqueness of every individual if there are only four basic natures represented in all of mankind?

Answer *There are still enormous opportunities for individuality, even within limited parameters. For example, in addition to the limited number of races on earth, there is also a limited number of skin tones and pigmentation (black, red, yellow or white), eye color (black, brown, blue or green), and hair shading and pigmentation (black, brown, red or blonde). Obviously, there is no chartreuse or hot pink hair in nature, yet, few would argue that with the unlimited DNA combinations that are possible, every human being is unique in appearance, even within limitations. The same individuality also exists within limited nature types, because of the vast DNA combinations available within each dominant and subdominant nature, as well as in the unique combinations of characteristics available from all of the four natures.*

Question How do the four types illustrated throughout Chapter One correspond with each other and with the four types represented on The Personality Compass?

Answer There are dozens of names for the four basic personality types. The following are just a few of the most well-known.

Historical Review of Nature Types					
Name	**Theory**	**Type**			
Hippocrates	Humors	Choleric	Melancholic	Phlegmatic	Sanguine
Aristotle	Opposites	Fire (Warm)	Earth (Dry)	Water (Moist)	Air (Cool)
Jung	Functions	Thinking	Intuition	Feeling	Sensation
	Attitudes	Extroverted	Judging	Introverted	Perceiving
Myers/ Briggs	Codes for Jung Types	ENTP, ENTJ ESTP, ESTJ	ENFJ, INTJ INTP, ISTJ	INFP, INFJ ISFP, ISFJ	ESFP, ESFJ ENFP, ISTP
Watson/ Crick	DNA Nucleotides	Adenine	Guanine	Cytosine	Thymine
Nomi/Besher	Blood Types	Blood Type O	Blood Type A	Blood Type AB	Blood Type B
Friedman/ Sperry	Chemical Type Split-BrainType	Type A	Left Brain	Type B	Right Brain
Abravanel/ King	Body Types	Pituitary	Adrenal	Gonadal	Thyroid
Mar	Facial Types	Square	Triangular	Round	Oblong
Mendel	Handwriting Type	AngularArcade	Garland	Thread	
Pavlov/ Lykken	Canine Types	Excitatory	Inhibitory	Steadfast	Energetic
Turner/Greco	Cultural Types	NORTH	EAST	SOUTH	WEST

Chapter Two

Introducing The
Personality Compass

The Cultural Analogy at a Glance

For centuries, referring to "the four corners of the earth" has been one way to allude to the north, east, south and west quadrants of our planet. Interestingly, the general cultures that developed within each of the four segments of the globe have acquired prevalent characteristics that are distinctive and recognizable throughout the world. We have certain perceptions in our minds that we associate with people from the North, from East cultures, from the South and people who live in the West.

When referring to the global hemispheres, the mental pictures and descriptions which have already been established in our minds regarding people from these four geographical regions would probably be very similar. In fact, when dozens of people from a variety of cultures, regions and backgrounds were asked to describe their perceptions of people from the northern, eastern, southern and western hemispheres, the similarities of their perceptions were uncanny. Identical adjectives were used in many cases.

Using what is already familiar, the Personality Compass pinpoints the NORTH nature or personality to characterize people who are fundamentally assertive, decisive and task-oriented. The EAST nature characterizes people who are highly structured, pay attention to detail and believe in following rules. The SOUTH nature characterizes easy-going people who enjoy spending time with, talking to and helping other people. The WEST nature characterizes people who are free-spirited, creative and who seek adventure.

The Personality Compass at a Glance

• Natural leader • Goal-centered • Fast-paced • Task-oriented • Assertive
• Decisive • Confident • Determined • Competitive • Independent
"Gets the Job Done Fast"

NORTH

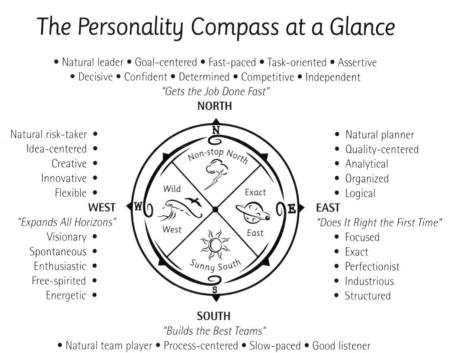

Natural risk-taker •
Idea-centered •
Creative •
Innovative •
Flexible •
WEST
"Expands All Horizons"
Visionary •
Spontaneous •
Enthusiastic •
Free-spirited •
Energetic •

• Natural planner
• Quality-centered
• Analytical
• Organized
• Logical
EAST
"Does It Right the First Time"
• Focused
• Exact
• Perfectionist
• Industrious
• Structured

SOUTH
"Builds the Best Teams"
• Natural team player • Process-centered • Slow-paced • Good listener
• Non-confrontational • Sensitive • Patient • Understanding • Generous •Helpful

Everyone will have some characteristics from all four nature types, but one type will
capture the personality's essence more accurately than the others. NORTH, EAST,
SOUTH, WEST. . . which of these describes you best?

NORTH Nature

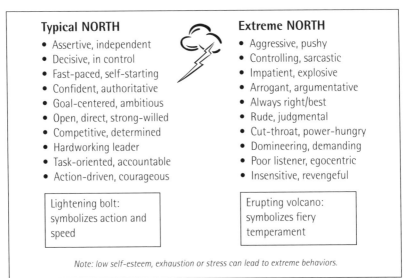

Typical NORTH

- Assertive, independent
- Decisive, in control
- Fast-paced, self-starting
- Confident, authoritative
- Goal-centered, ambitious
- Open, direct, strong-willed
- Competitive, determined
- Hardworking leader
- Task-oriented, accountable
- Action-driven, courageous

Extreme NORTH

- Aggressive, pushy
- Controlling, sarcastic
- Impatient, explosive
- Arrogant, argumentative
- Always right/best
- Rude, judgmental
- Cut-throat, power-hungry
- Domineering, demanding
- Poor listener, egocentric
- Insensitive, revengeful

Lightening bolt:
symbolizes action and
speed

Erupting volcano:
symbolizes fiery
temperament

Note: low self-esteem, exhaustion or stress can lead to extreme behaviors.

The North Culture Analogy

People living in the cultural North (think of the robust Icelanders) share certain qualities which are common to our collective consciousness of North cultural characteristics. Perhaps related to the cold, harsh climate which makes survival a struggle, NORTH attributes incorporate strength, decisiveness and the competitive determination to tackle a tough job and get it done fast.

EAST Nature

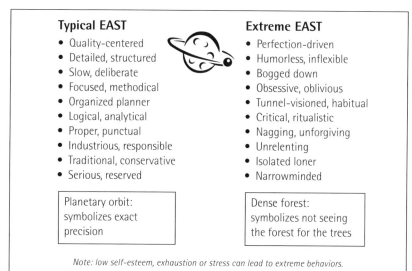

Typical EAST

- Quality-centered
- Detailed, structured
- Slow, deliberate
- Focused, methodical
- Organized planner
- Logical, analytical
- Proper, punctual
- Industrious, responsible
- Traditional, conservative
- Serious, reserved

Planetary orbit:
symbolizes exact
precision

Extreme EAST

- Perfection-driven
- Humorless, inflexible
- Bogged down
- Obsessive, oblivious
- Tunnel-visioned, habitual
- Critical, ritualistic
- Nagging, unforgiving
- Unrelenting
- Isolated loner
- Narrowminded

Dense forest:
symbolizes not seeing
the forest for the trees

Note: low self-esteem, exhaustion or stress can lead to extreme behaviors.

The East Culture Analogy

People living in the cultural East (think of the decorous, ceremonial Chinese) also share a number of common denominators. Their cultures follow traditions and protocol. Eastern art and architecture are often intricately detailed and reflect a sense of order. EAST qualities include caution, organization and discipline, perhaps because the early populations which emerged created the need to avoid chaos.

SOUTH Nature

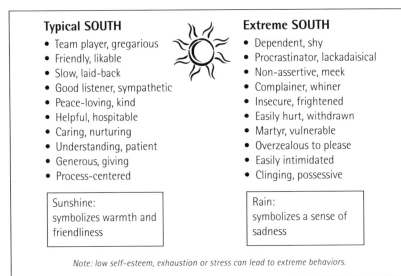

Typical SOUTH
- Team player, gregarious
- Friendly, likable
- Slow, laid-back
- Good listener, sympathetic
- Peace-loving, kind
- Helpful, hospitable
- Caring, nurturing
- Understanding, patient
- Generous, giving
- Process-centered

Sunshine:
symbolizes warmth and friendliness

Extreme SOUTH
- Dependent, shy
- Procrastinator, lackadaisical
- Non-assertive, meek
- Complainer, whiner
- Insecure, frightened
- Easily hurt, withdrawn
- Martyr, vulnerable
- Overzealous to please
- Easily intimidated
- Clinging, possessive

Rain:
symbolizes a sense of sadness

Note: low self-esteem, exhaustion or stress can lead to extreme behaviors.

The South Culture Analogy

People living in the cultural South (think of the affable, laid-back Australians) also share specific similarities. Southern cultures are caring and friendly, and often reflect the cooperative spirit of an agrarian culture which historically depended on people listening to each other, working together and lending a helping hand. SOUTHS display the sunny warmth of the tropics because they genuinely enjoy people.

WEST Nature

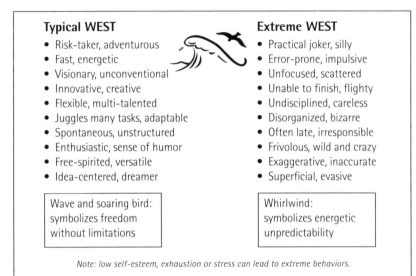

Typical WEST
- Risk-taker, adventurous
- Fast, energetic
- Visionary, unconventional
- Innovative, creative
- Flexible, multi-talented
- Juggles many tasks, adaptable
- Spontaneous, unstructured
- Enthusiastic, sense of humor
- Free-spirited, versatile
- Idea-centered, dreamer

Wave and soaring bird:
symbolizes freedom
without limitations

Extreme WEST
- Practical joker, silly
- Error-prone, impulsive
- Unfocused, scattered
- Unable to finish, flighty
- Undisciplined, careless
- Disorganized, bizarre
- Often late, irresponsible
- Frivolous, wild and crazy
- Exaggerative, inaccurate
- Superficial, evasive

Whirlwind:
symbolizes energetic
unpredictability

Note: low self-esteem, exhaustion or stress can lead to extreme behaviors.

The West Culture Analogy

People living in the cultural West (think of the adventurous, open-minded Americans) also share many cultural characteristics. The "wild West" spirit is at the heart of the West culture. Their environment reflects the wide open spaces without barriers, with a history of settlers and rebels heading out on yet uncharted paths. Themes of freedom and promises of adventure reflect the risk-taking and visionary WEST nature.

Easy Ways to Identify Personality Type

Finding the Weakest Link in the Personality Chain

It is often easier to identify the weakest nature of your personality first. You will quickly recognize:

- what you do not like
- what you fear
- what you tend to avoid
- what makes you feel uncomfortable
- what you do not do well
- what you do not enjoy

Once you know your weakest nature in the personality chain, you know without a doubt that your dominant personality type will be the opposite.

Review the preceding charts of qualities and talents to identify your own or another's weakest nature. Use the diagrams on the following page to understand visually that your dominant type will inevitably appear opposite your weakest link in the chain on the Personality Compass.

Knowing Your Weaknesses Helps Pinpoint Your Strengths

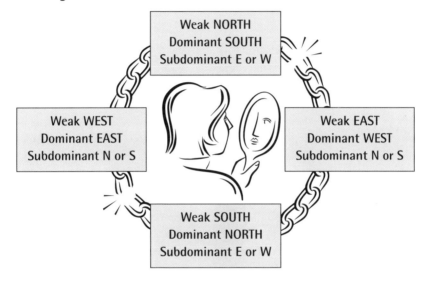

Weak NORTH
Dominant SOUTH
Subdominant E or W

Weak WEST
Dominant EAST
Subdominant N or S

Weak EAST
Dominant WEST
Subdominant N or S

Weak SOUTH
Dominant NORTH
Subdominant E or W

Recognizing your weakest link reveals the qualities and talents you need to develop most in order to be well-rounded, improve your relationships and increase your career success.

The Importance of Knowing Your Top 2 Types: Your Dyad

Identifying Your Dyad Leads to Self-discovery
Understanding your dominant (1) and subdominant (2) natures (your dyad) is important in two ways.

- It gives you a clear grasp of the range of your most prevalent strengths and talents.

- It helps you know the qualities and skills that are your weakest links, which, of course, you need to develop in order to achieve the highest possible degree of success in your relationships and career.

Identifying Another Person's Dyad Leads to Effective Communication
Paula, a dominant EAST-subdominant SOUTH (ES), knew that Mr Everett, her boss, was an EAST-NORTH. She planned the strategies for her coming meeting with him very carefully. He would, as an EAST, expect her to have detailed reports, complete with logical charts, graphs and analyses ready to distribute in quality binders. She knew also that she must fight her SOUTH tendency to chit-chat and occasionally get off the subject, and she must remember to get right to the essential data he wanted and then listen to what his NORTH had to say.

Tuning In to Your Top 3 Types: Your Triad

How the Triad Works

- Your dominant type (1) will always be the opposite of your weakest link (4).

- Both your subdominant (2) and your third highest type (3) will always be adjacent to your dominant type on the Personality Compass.

- Your top three types (your triad) may be nearly equal in strengths and competence, or they may be clearly unequal, depending upon various factors such as genetics, environment and upbringing.

- The more equal and balanced you are in all of your top three types, your triad, the more difficult it will be to determine their order of dominance; however, by identifying your weakest link first, your dominant type will easily stand out as that which is opposite.

- It is important to know your top three types and your weakest link because it helps you evaluate the entire spectrum of your strengths and weaknesses so that you can make more enlightened choices when choosing a mate or a career path.

Using the Triad to Make Critical Decisions

Marcus, a university student, couldn't decide whether he wanted to become a pediatrician or an architect. Both appealed to him. After identifying his triad as NW-E, the choice was easier. With SOUTH as his weakest link, and EAST as his third type in the triad, he clearly would not be as happy dealing with children all day in a structured office environment as he would exploring site locations and using his imagination to bring a creative vision to life as a NORTH-WEST.

The Compass Challenge:
Type Identification Exercises

A few challenging questions will now give you the opportunity to fine-tune your knowledge and understanding of each personality type. Circle your choice.

What Would You Choose?

If you had to choose between (a) going to a job you enjoy, or (b) chatting for a couple of hours with acquaintances on the patio, what would you choose?
NORTH would choose to work. SOUTH would choose the conversation.

If you had to choose between (a) finishing your calculations for a report you've been working on, or b) dropping everything immediately to go parasailing, what would you choose?
EAST would choose to finish what they're doing. WEST would choose adventure over tedium.

If you had to choose between (a) helping someone else look good, or b) taking credit for the hard work you put into making a project successful, what would you choose?
SOUTH would choose to stay in the background and let others receive the accolades. NORTH would choose to do the work themselves and receive the recognition they deserve.

If you had to choose between (a) coming up with creative ideas for a huge stage production number, or (b) coming up with a step-by-step procedure manual for first-year medical students, which would you choose?

WEST would choose to think creatively and be part of an exciting and chaotic environment. EAST would choose to think sequentially and be part of a quiet and structured environment.

Making More Choices

Type Identification Exercise

If you have already determined that you are a dominant NORTH (a) would you choose to stay mostly in one place and maintain a sense of routine, or (b) would you prefer to work outside or travel a great deal?

NORTH-EASTS would choose to stay in a stable, secure environment. NORTH-WESTS would choose an environment of change and unpredictability.

If you have already determined that you are a dominant EAST, (a) would you choose opportunities to be in charge of other people and make important decisions for them, or (b) would you prefer to have someone else in charge and not have the burden of having to make decisions on your shoulders?

EAST-NORTHS would choose opportunities for leadership and authentic authority. EAST-SOUTHS would choose to let others be in control.

If you have already determined that you are a dominant SOUTH, (a) would you choose to help others plan specific strategies for raising funds for a new hospital, or (b) would you prefer to design the building and coordinate its on-site construction?

SOUTH-EASTS would choose to be involved in the planning stages of the community project. SOUTH-WESTS would prefer to be in the middle of its actual creation.

If you have already determined that you are a dominant WEST, (a) would you choose to work alone to prioritize the problem-solving tasks that must be completed prior to a committee meeting, or (b) would you prefer to be part of a team effort to motivate the people on your committee to work together?

WEST-NORTHS would choose to work alone on deciding the tasks that need to be done by a deadline. WEST-SOUTHS would prefer to work as part of a cohesive team to get diverse people to want to work together cooperatively with each other.

Making Even More Choices

Type Identification Exercise

Directions: place a cross (X) *in the blank next to the statements below which most closely reflect your preferences, or your perceived preferences, of the person you are attempting to identify, according to nature and personality.*

The person I am trying to identify would rather . . .

1. ___ Talk to anyone who will listen about a challenging new project (N)
   ___ Come up with a detailed plan to ensure the success of a project (E)
   ___ Listen to friends who need to talk about their exciting projects (S)
   ___ Come up with ten ideas for possible future projects (W)
2. ___ Be in charge of a committee (N)
   ___ Keep accurate minutes of a committee meeting (E)
   ___ Be a regular member of a committee (S)
   ___ Be on as few committees as possible (W)
3. ___ Receive public recognition for all that they do (N)
   ___ Be recognized without a fuss for competence and quality (E)
   ___ Work behind the scenes without public recognition (S)
   ___ Be recognized for a creative sense of humor (W)
4. ___ Spend time working on an important project (N)
   ___ Spend time reading a mentally challenging book (E)
   ___ Spend time talking on the telephone to an acquaintance (S)
   ___ Spend time playing a physically challenging game (W)

5 ___ Work alone than work with people who move slowly (N)
___ Work alone than work with people who rush (E)
___ Work with others than work alone any time (S)
___ Work with others, but only if they're fun to work with (W)

6 ___ Start and finish an assignment as fast as possible (N)
___ Start and finish an assignment after careful thought (E)
___ Not rush to start or finish an assignment right away (S)
___ Start an assignment fast, but not hurry to finish (W)

7 ___ Work than take a vacation (N)
___ Plan a short vacation in detail (E)
___ Take a vacation than work any time (S)
___ Take off on an unplanned vacation (W)

8 ___ Challenge time (N)
___ Be on time (E)
___ Forget about time (S)
___ Have a good time (W)

9 ___ Fight than give up a goal (N)
___ Reach a goal in a step-by-step sequence (E)
___ Give up a goal than face a conflict (S)
___ Change goals often, whether reached or not (W)

10 ___ Have the authority to make quick decisions (N)
___ Be involved in covert decision-making (E)
___ Be part of a team decision (S)
___ Not have to make a definitive decision (W)

Which Type Has These Talents?

Type Identification Exercise

Directions: place a N, E, S, or W in the blank which identifies the talent. The distinction between which types might excel in these areas is never clearly defined, but it is interesting to consider from the perspective of a person's basic nature.

	Talent	Type
1	Measures precisely	____
2	Makes quick decisions	____
3	Checks for errors	____
4	Builds cohesive teams	____
5	Adapts to change	____
6	Solves problems	____
7	Takes charge	____
8	Listens intently	____
9	Keeps accurate records	____
10	Unites diverse groups	____
11	Juggles many tasks	____
12	Leads a group	____
13	Organizes data	____
14	Brainstorms new ideas	____
15	Meets deadlines	____
16.	Analyzes logically	____

	Talent	**Type**
17	Empowers others	_____
18	Mediates a conflict	_____
19	Asserts authority	_____
20	Motivates people	_____
21	Plans in detail	_____
22	Creates new methods	_____
23	Speeds up processes	_____
24	Cooperates unselfishly	_____

Answers: 1 E; 2 N; 3 E; 4 S; 5 W; 6 W; 7 N; 8 S; 9 E; 10 S; 11 W; 12 N; 13 E; 14 W; 15 N; 16 E; 17 S; 18 S; 19 N; 20 W; 21 E; 22 W; 23 N; 24 S

Which Type Makes the Best Role Model As a . . . ?

Type Identification Exercise

Directions: place a N, E, S, *or* W *in the blank which identifies the role. The distinction between which types might excel in these areas is never clearly defined, but it is interesting to consider from the perspective of a person's basic nature.*

	Role	Type
1	Friend	_____
2	Wheeler-dealer	_____
3	Expert	_____
4	Leader	_____
5	Motivator	_____
6	Competitor	_____
7	Persuader	_____
8	Record-keeper	_____
9	Teacher	_____
10	Comedian	_____
11	Planner	_____
12	Conversationalist	_____
13	Decision-maker	_____
14	Risk-taker	_____
15	Commander	_____
16	Volunteer	_____

	Role	**Type**
17	Inspector	_____
18	Caretaker	_____
19	Thrill-seeker	_____
20	Realist	_____
21	Negotiator	_____
22	Team player	_____
23	Inventor	_____
24	Organizer	_____

Answers: 1 S; 2 W; 3 E; 4 N; 5 W; 6 N; 7 E; 8 E; 9 S; 10 W; 11 E; 12 S; 13 N; 14 W; 15 N; 16 S; 17 E; 18 S; 19 W; 20 N; 21 N; 22 S; 23 W; 24 E

37

Which Type Is Attracted to These Hobbies?

Type Identification Exercise

Directions: place a N, E, S, or W in the blank which identifies the hobby. The distinction between which types might excel in these areas is never clearly defined, but it is interesting to consider from the perspective of a person's basic nature.

	Hobby	Type
1	Playing golf	_____
2	Ballet dancing	_____
3	Gambling	_____
4	Horseback riding	_____
5	Helping the community	_____
6	Playing football	_____
7	Fly-fishing	_____
8	Acting	_____
9	Lifeguarding	_____
10	Playing bridge	_____
11	Teaching Sunday school	_____
12	Oil painting	_____
13	Talking on the telephone	_____
14	Hospital volunteering	_____
15	Animal training	_____
16	Playing the piano	_____

Hobby	Type
17 Skydiving	____
18 Riding motorcycles	____
19 Practicing martial arts	____
20 Feeding the homeless	____
21 Baking cookies	____
22 Racing	____
23 Reading	____
24 Scuba diving	____

Which Type Is Motivated By . . . ?

Type Identification Exercise

Directions: place a N, E, S, or W in the blank which identifies the motivational turn-on. The distinction between which types might be motivated by these factors is never clearly defined, but it is interesting to consider from the perspective of a person's basic nature.

	Motivational Turn-ons	Type
1	Cooperation	_____
2	Goals	_____
3	Quality	_____
4	Overt praise	_____
5	Feeling needed	_____
6	Freedom	_____
7	Efficiency	_____
8	Imagination	_____
9	Camaraderie	_____
10	Competition	_____
11	Power and control	_____
12	Friendliness	_____
13	Adventure	_____
14	Constant change	_____
15	Structure	_____

	Motivational Turn-ons	Type
16	Optimism	____
17	Spontaneity	____
18	Making decisions	____
19	Creative ideas	____
20	Logical analysis	____
21	Teamwork	____
22	Having authority	____
23	Good manners	____
24	Organization	____

Which Type Performs These Jobs Best ?

Type Identification Exercise

Directions: place a N, E, S, or W in the blank which identifies job preference. The distinction between which types might excel in these areas is never clearly defined, but it is interesting to consider from the perspective of a person's basic nature.

	Job Competence/Title	Type
1	Salesperson	_____
2	Quality Control Manager	_____
3	Interior Designer	_____
4	Minister	_____
5	Coach	_____
6	Chief Executive	_____
7	Accountant	_____
8	Computer Programmer	_____
9	Teacher	_____
10	Architect	_____
11	Explorer	_____
12	President	_____
13	Researcher	_____
14	Tour Guide	_____
15	Nurse	_____
16	Counselor	_____

Job Competence/Title	Type
17 Professor	____
18 Pilot	____
19 Entertainer	____
20 Military Officer	____
21 Brain Surgeon	____
22 Diplomat	____
23 Head Chef	____
24 Negotiator	____

Answers: 1 S; 2 E; 3 W; 4 S; 5 N; 6 N; 7 E; 8 E; 9 S; 10 W; 11 W; 12 N; 13 E; 14 W; 15 S; 16 S; 17 E; 18 E; 19 W; 20 N; 21 E; 22 S; 23 N; 24 N

43

Which Skills Do You Need for These Situations?

Type Identification Exercise

Directions: no matter what type you are, you can learn to handle situations appropriately. Identify the best type of response for each situation by placing a N, E, S, or W in the blank which identifies the situational type.

	Situation	Direction to Go
1	Someone pays you a compliment	Go ____
2	You're put in charge of a committee	Go ____
3	A friend asks you for your ideas	Go ____
4	A detailed report is due for your job	Go ____
5	Someone accuses you wrongly	Go ____
6	Your place settings must be perfect	Go ____
7	Your cooperation and teamwork are required	Go ____
8	You need to make a decision now	Go ____
9	A friend says drop everything and come along	Go ____
10	You're caught in the middle of a fight	Go ____
11	You must negotiate a contract	Go ____
12	Your priorities need to be established	Go ____
13	Your friend needs a shoulder to cry on	Go ____
14	You need to motivate apathetic people	Go ____
15	Your shelves must be organized	Go ____
16	You must cut through confusion and chaos	Go ____

Situation	Direction to Go
17 It is important that you listen to all sides	Go _____
18 Someone threatens your authority	Go _____
19 You must wear the perfect outfit	Go _____
20 You are hosting a large party	Go _____
21 Following the recipe exactly is critical	Go _____
22 You need bottom-line results fast	Go _____
23 Someone asks you to try mountain-climbing	Go _____
24 Someone needs help with the dishes	Go _____

Answers: 1 S; 2 N; 3 W; 4 E; 5 N; 6 E; 7 S; 8 N; 9 W; 10 S; 11 N; 12 N; 13 S; 14 W; 15 E; 16 E; 17 S; 18 N; 19 E; 20 W; 21 E; 22 N; 23 W; 24 S

45

Quick-Test for Type

Are You More NORTH or SOUTH?

Directions: read the choices below and choose the word that describes you more often than the other (even though you may have both characteristics). Circle A or B for each grouping of choices and tally your score on the following page.

1 A Confident
   B Helpful
2 A Self-reliant
   B Understanding
3 A Fast-paced
   B Easy-going
4 A Independent
   B Team player
5 A Decisive
   B Diplomatic
6 A Assertive
   B Non-confrontational
7 A Competitive
   B Cooperative
8 A Strong-willed
   B Tolerant
9 A Leader
   B Loyal

10 A Goal-centered
    B People-centered
11 A Initiator
    B Listener
12 A Determined
    B Unselfish
13 A Straightforward
    B Patient
14 A Results-focused
    B Relationship-focused
15 A Hardworking
    B Friendly
16 A In-charge
    B Generous
17 A Task-oriented
    B Peace-oriented
18 A Authoritative
    B Considerate

19 A Bold
    B Supportive
20 A Productive
    B Faithful
21 A Self-starter
    B Volunteer
22 A Autocratic
    B Accommodating
23 A Directive
    B Sociable
24 A Opinionated
    B Sensitive
25 A Challenger
    B Mediator
26 A Doer
    B Communicator
27 A Deadline-driven
    B Values-driven

| 28 A Tough | 29 A Driver | 30 A Achiever |
| B Appreciative | B Pleaser | B Caregiver |

Total As_____

Total Bs_____

47

Quick-Test for Type

Are You More EAST or WEST?

Directions: read the choices below and choose the word that describes you more often than the other (even though you may have both characteristics). Circle C or D for each grouping of choices and tally your score on the following page.

1	C Organized D Creative	10	C Traditional D Risk-taker	19	C Persistent D Imaginative
2	C Structured D Flexible	11	C Factual D Fun-loving	20	C Cautious D Open-minded
3	C Quality-centered D Idea-centered	12	C Analytical D Cheerful	21	C Finisher D Motivator
4	C Cultured D Enthusiastic	13	C Consistent D Versatile	22	C Rule-follower D Option-provider
5	C Logical D Visionary	14	C Serious D Humorous	23	C Systematic D Carefree
6	C Reserved D Innovative	15	C Efficient D Dreamer	24	C Precise D Inventive
7	C Planner D Spontaneous	16	C Punctual D Daring	25	C Standard-setter D Coordinator
8	C Focused D Resourceful	17	C Reliable D Delegator	26	C Persuasive D Adventurous
9	C Perfectionist D Free-spirited	18	C Industrious D Improvising	27	C Protocol-focused D Methods-focused

| 28 C Accurate | 29 C Double-checker | 30 C Record-keeper |
| D Adaptable | D Wheeler-dealer | D Trend-setter |

Total Cs_____

Total Ds_____

Now that you have identified your top two groups of personality strengths, review both lists of characteristics carefully. You will know which of the two clusters of traits is stronger in your nature than the other. Fill that in below as your Dominant Type. Fill in your second strongest nature as your Subdominant Type. (Note: your dominant nature will always be opposite your weakest type on the Personality Compass.)

Dominant Type_____ Subdominant Type_____

Questions & Answers About the Personality Compass

Question What are the advantages of using the Personality Compass over other personality typing systems?

Answer *The five major advantages of using the Personality Compass are as follows.*

1 *It is based on concepts and terminology that are already familiar, so new information does not have to be learned.*

2 *Because there is already a natural connection between adjacent compass directions (such as NE/NW, SE/SW), it is easy to understand the natural connection between dominant and subdominant personality types that are adjacent on the Personality Compass.*

3 *Knowing both the dominant and subdominant natures of an individual reveals far more about that person than having limited knowledge of the dominant type only.*

4 *Understanding that N, E, S and W are simply names for directions, with no hierarchy of importance or value, makes it easy to see that the same is true for the four different, but equally valuable, personality types.*

5 *The graphic Personality Compass helps to simplify the complexity of human behavior and personality so that you can quickly understand how to please, motivate, employ and avoid conflict with specific individuals by understanding their nature type.*

Question   Doesn't the Personality Compass stereotype Northerners, Easterners, Southerners and Westerners, without allowing for the uniqueness of individuals within each geographical region and culture?

Answer   *The Personality Compass neither claims nor implies that all people living within a particular region or culture are the same. However, there are certain characteristics that have become recognized and accepted as typical of people from a particular region or culture. It has nothing to do with where one lives, since a NORTH, EAST, SOUTH or WEST nature could live in any geographical location or culture and still exhibit those universally understood cultural characteristics.*

Question   At a time in history when cultural diversity is a major issue, doesn't the Personality Compass promote homogeneous grouping of people?

Answer   *On the contrary, the Personality Compass emphasizes the positive aspects of cultural differences, as well as similarities, and encourages people to develop the unique and advantageous strengths of each culture and its analogous nature. The more characteristics we can develop from all of the four natures, the more well-rounded and competent we will become. Although our basic nature and personality is innate within each of us, we can learn to overcome our weaknesses and develop the inherent strengths of every nature. The Personality Compass explains how to do that.*

Chapter Three

Valuing the Nature of NORTH

The Uniqueness of NORTH

Typical NORTH
- Assertive, independent
- Decisive, in control
- Fast-paced, self-starting
- Confident, authoritative
- Goal-centered, ambitious
- Open, direct, strong-willed
- Competitive, determined
- Hardworking leader
- Task-oriented, accountable
- Action-driven, courageous

Extreme NORTH
- Aggressive, pushy
- Controlling, sarcastic
- Impatient, explosive
- Arrogant, argumentative
- Always right/best
- Rude, judgmental
- Cutthroat, power-hungry
- Domineering, demanding
- Poor listener, egocentric
- Insensitive, revengeful

NORTHS at a Glance

"NORTHS Do It with Confidence"

- **Motto** NORTHS get the job done fast
- **Symbol** Lightning bolt
- **Greatest strength** Making quick decisions
- **Basic weakness** Impatience
- **Fundamental aptitude** Leadership
- **Priority** Goals
- **Motivational turn-on** Competition
- **Pet peeve** Indecision
- **Work and play style** Independent
- **Main work competency** Supervisory
- **Pace** Fast and determined
- **Image** Achievement

NORTH Role Model

The story is told that when Lee Iacocca decided that Chrysler should have a convertible, and the engineering department told him it would take nearly a year to build the prototype, Iacocca exclaimed, "Go get a car and saw the top off the damn thing!"

Top 10 Super Strengths of NORTHS

Typical NORTHS might often exhibit:

1. Leadership
2. Determination
3. Confidence
4. Know-how
5. Drive
6. Speed
7. Courage
8. Initiative
9. Willpower
10. Accountability

NORTHS Can Take Charge

Frank is a NORTH commercial airline pilot who recently saved dozens of lives while taking charge of rescuing attempts after his plane crashed in a field. He was later described by one of the passengers as "tireless and unrelenting, a man with a mission who knew just what needed to be done, and who told people exactly what they needed to do to help."

From Super Strengths to Team Stars

How NORTHS Charge-Up a Team

Most NORTHS naturally help the teams they are on by:

- Building team confidence
- Motivating team players to work hard and put in long hours
- Raising individual and team competitive levels
- Increasing team productivity
- Developing team speed
- Turning individual apathy into team action
- Keeping each player accountable for reaching the team goal
- Instilling team determination to excel
- Inspiring their team to expect success
- Leading/coaching their team to victory

When NORTH Team Leadership Works Best

The NORTH authoritarian leadership style is most effective when:

- dependent or inexperienced individuals or teams need someone to tell them exactly what to do and how to do it;
- hostile or out-of-control individuals or teams need someone to take charge and be strong and assertive to maintain order and get them on track.

Top 10 Danger Zones of NORTHS

Extreme NORTHS might often exhibit:

1 Intolerance
2 Intimidation
3 Manipulation
4 Belligerence
5 Impatience
6 Insensitivity
7 Arrogance
8 Chauvinism
9 Obstinance
10 Bossiness

NORTHS Can Take Over

On a bad day, George is an unpopular store manager who storms around the floor and embarrasses his employees when things aren't the way he wants. When he's upset, he doesn't want to hear suggestions and he doesn't want help. One worker said of him, "George expects people to do what he says when he says it, without any questions. He wants total control . . . or else!"

From Danger Zones to Dynamite

- NORTH *intolerance* and *intimidation* can sometimes result in improved performance and/or service.

  When someone is performing below the standards and expectations of their job, or when someone is providing intolerable service, NORTHS can let them know it and demand improvements in no uncertain terms.

- NORTH *manipulation* and *belligerence* can sometimes result in overcoming major obstacles.

  When roadblocks appear to make goals unattainable, NORTHS can get angry enough to find seemingly impossible ways to get what they want.

- NORTH *impatience* and *insensitivity* can sometimes result in ending complaints before they have a chance to escalate.

  When people begin to whine and complain about things that are going wrong, particularly if they start to slow down the work process, NORTHS can nip it in the bud with no regrets.

- NORTH *arrogance* and *chauvinism* can sometimes result in undermining the opposition's confidence.

  When it is important to maintain confidence and a competitive edge, no one can do it like NORTHS , as they can cut opponents down to size with only a look, a gesture or a word.

- NORTH *obstinance* and *bossiness* can sometimes result in getting the job done on time or ahead of schedule.

  When there is a deadline to meet, NORTHS will go to any lengths to meet it, and they won't hesitate to tell others how to get the job done fast.

Understanding the Differences Between NORTH-EASTS and NORTH-WESTS

The Personality Compass analogy between the North, East, South and West cultures and the four cultural natures makes it easy to identify and remember the natural qualities and competencies of people within each dominant compass direction. However, think how much more we can know about people who are dominant in the NORTH direction if we can also identify their subdominant nature, which is to be found adjacent on the Personality Compass.

Greg and Molly: Alike and Different

Greg, a dominant NORTH-subdominant EAST, has the most qualities in common with North cultures, and the second highest number of qualities in common with East cultures. Molly, a dominant NORTH who is sub-dominant WEST, has much in common with Greg because of their shared NORTH qualities. Yet Greg and Molly are different in many ways, too, because of their opposite subdominant natures.

Knowing both the dominant and subdominant nature can have a significant impact on the types of tasks that appeal to an individual, as well as on the aptitudes required to achieve quality and excellence at the tasks. Greg, a NORTH-EAST, is assertive, decisive, structured, detailed and organized. Molly, a NORTH-WEST, is assertive, decisive, flexible, creative and adventurous. They would have somewhat differing interests and talents, and would not be equally suited to the same job, even though both are dominant NORTHS.

NORTH-EAST People

Assertive • Decisive • Structured • Detailed • Organized

NORTH-WEST People

Assertive • Decisive • Flexible • Creative • Adventurous

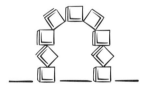

Recognizing NORTH Behaviors

Twenty or more crosses (X) *indicate a strong NORTH nature.*

NORTHS in general . . .

- [ ] Talk, move and eat fast
- [ ] Look people directly in the eye
- [ ] Shake hands firmly
- [ ] Speak boldly and with authority
- [ ] Sound like they mean what they say
- [ ] Hold their head high and shoulders back
- [ ] Stand tall and use sweeping gestures
- [ ] Take large, heavy steps
- [ ] Wear strong colors and styles
- [ ] Exhibit high energy and endurance
- [ ] Move with a sense of purpose
- [ ] Appear confident and in control
- [ ] Seem courageous and fearless
- [ ] Discuss issues that are important to them

- [ ] Work for fun
- [ ] Hate to waste time
- [ ] Prefer talking to listening
- [ ] Enjoy attention and praise
- [ ] Act first and think later
- [ ] Like to be in charge

- [ ] Put goals as a top priority
- [ ] Find excuses intolerable
- [ ] Confront conflicts head-on
- [ ] Ignore small talk
- [ ] Can be intimidating to non-NORTHS
- [ ] Are insensitive to others' feelings at times
- [ ] Become angry in traffic or other tie-ups
- [ ] Know what they want and what to do
- [ ] Feel they are right much of the time

- [ ] Respect high achievers
- [ ] Compete in almost anything
- [ ] Play to win
- [ ] Make quick, firm decisions
- [ ] Value success, power and speed

Recognizing NORTH Children

Typical NORTH Children in General . . .

- Let you know what they want in a hurry
- Eat, drink and move fast
- Determine their own bedtime
- Tell other children what to do
- Play well independently
- Ignore the word "no" when possible
- Try to walk early
- Need to be kept busy
- Make their own rules
- Like school and its competitive activities

Dillon had a mind of his own almost from the moment of his birth. If he didn't get fed at the first sign of hunger, he screamed, red-faced, until his needs were met. If he sensed he was missing out on something, he fought sleep in spite of his exhaustion. Yet, he had a zest for trying to crawl or walk, or climb to the top of the jungle gym, that was exciting to watch and an inspiration to anyone tempted to slow down or take a rest.

Extreme NORTH Children in General . . .
- Are under some degree of stress
- Throw temper tantrums frequently
- Refuse to do what they don't want to do
- Are obstinate about their likes and dislikes
- Become impatient with anything slow
- Fight to have their own way
- Become demanding and rude
- Try to control situations and people
- Dislike school because they dislike authority
- Insist on having the best toy

When Shane didn't like his food, it wasn't enough to make a face – he would spit it as far as he could, preferably with a human target in mind. If another child was playing with a toy he wanted, Shane had no qualms about snatching it from him. In fact, he would often grab a toy that he had previously rejected just because another child had chosen to play with it.

Recognizing NORTHS in Different Roles

As Students
NORTHS in General . . .

- Know the answers frequently
- Express opinions openly
- Take a firm position on issues or ideas
- Prefer being "right" to being "popular"
- Challenge the instructor's knowledge
- Are usually in the middle of the action
- Find ways to get attention
- Get bored when work is slow and quiet
- Compete for top honors or recognition
- Do extra work just to stay busy
- Enjoy giving presentations in front of the class
- Play hard at break, games or gym class

As Athletes
NORTHS in General . . .

- Believe in their ability to be the best
- Train hard to be in top physical condition
- Push physical and mental endurance to the limits
- Play or compete to win
- Are generally poor losers
- Get angry with people who impede their victory
- Insist on a tough work ethic in teammates
- Refuse to give up trying to reach goals
- Overcome huge odds through sheer determination
- Intimidate fellow competitors by strength of will
- Will question coaches if they disagree with strategies
- Exhibit personal pride

As Leaders
NORTHS in General . . .

- Employ an authoritarian leadership style
- Are confident about how things should be done
- Put in long hours without being asked
- Take charge in a crisis and expect to be followed
- Assert control to achieve goals
- Make tough decisions without fear of reprisals
- Do not tolerate excuses or wasting time
- Rarely ask for help
- Cut breaks short to get back to work
- Give orders more often than requests
- Have little interest in their own popularity
- Reward initiative and courage in others

As Friends, Spouses or Parents
NORTHS in General . . .

- Like to be the hub around which others turn
- Determine the general course of most relationships
- Provide strong shoulders to lean on
- Have answers and solutions when needed
- Are dependable in crises
- Feel closest to those who admire and praise them
- Can usually get others to do what they want
- Would rather spend money than time on people
- Measure success by accomplishments
- Enjoy being able to boast about loved ones (and themselves)
- May have conflict with people who defy them
- Express opinions more easily than feelings

Recognizing NORTHS in Different Situations

At Home
NORTHS in General . . .

- Provide a sense of security that they can do it all
- Work, play and love with passion
- Need to be "head of the household"
- Call most of the shots, openly or behind the scenes
- Get fidgety easily and find it hard to relax
- Like things to be done their way
- Forget to ask about everyone else's day
- Enjoy choosing the vacation spots
- Ask others to bring them what they want
- Interrupt when others are talking
- Are strong disciplinarians
- Save the day in emergencies

In a Social Environment
NORTHS in General . . .

- Stand out in a crowd
- Have an aura of importance
- Control topics of conversation
- Move around with purpose and confidence
- Seek out people of status to associate with
- Ignore people who don't interest them
- Mix business with pleasure
- Demand fast service and fast action
- Might order for everyone
- Leave big, impressive tips
- Arrive in a showy car
- Leave if they get bored or have nothing to gain

During an Interview
NORTHS in General . . .

- Are on time, but only a few minutes early
- Look others directly in the eye
- Shake hands firmly, sometimes too firmly
- Take a seat without being told
- Speak confidently, often about themselves
- Share their accomplishments openly
- Show interest in promotional opportunities
- Can be heard easily
- Ask about the tasks they would be performing if hired
- Talk about their future goals
- Appear comfortable, even bold
- May interview the interviewer a bit

On the Job
NORTHS in General . . .

- Do everything fast
- Compete to finish tasks first
- Get jobs done ahead of schedule
- Ask for more work to do, or just do it
- Offer unsolicited suggestions
- Get impatient with slow workers or procedures
- Take shortcuts, with or without permission
- Prefer to work independently
- Like to get or take credit when things go well
- Are ambitious to reach positions of authority
- Can be a bit bossy
- Demand a lot of themselves and others

Common Comments That Recognize Typical NORTHS

"My boss has it all. She's competent, and she always appears totally confident and in control. I've never seen her 'cop out' on the tough negotiations and decisions, and she's highly respected by her peers. I almost envy her success."

Bob T.

"Mac is amazing! He completed a $200 million project six weeks ahead of schedule, led the biggest alumni fund-raiser in our university's history, and coached his son's soccer team to the state championship!"

Ed J.

"Our daughter was determined to walk down the aisle by herself to receive her diploma. The doctors told her after the accident that the odds were against her – but she worked day and night for two years, and she beat the odds. When she reached that podium, she received a standing ovation for overcoming such tremendous obstacles to achieve her goal."

Mike and Laura K.

Common Comments That Recognize Extreme NORTHS

"*Every time my husband gets in the car, he starts honking the horn and yelling at drivers who go too slow, or block the passing lane, or don't give a turn signal. He gets so angry, I'm afraid he'll have a heart attack.*"

Becky R.

"*My wife will get up and get herself a snack during a commercial, and then sit back down beside me without bringing me anything. She says she doesn't think about it – that she assumes I'll tell her if I want something – but it really makes me wonder if she cares about me.*"

Tom P.

"*Our neighbor is so obnoxious! He's such a know-it-all. And not only does he know everything, but his stuff is better than anyone else's, he's been more places, done more things, and knows more important people. We secretly refer to him as 'Mr Been There, Done That.'*"

Freddy and Helen L.

Motivating NORTHS for Success

Tell NORTHS that it can't be done, and they will find a way to meet the challenge. Tell them you admire and respect how quickly they get things accomplished, and they will accomplish twice as much at twice the speed. Tell them you need their suggestions, and NORTHS will tell you exactly what should be done, how to do it, and who can do it best and fastest, or they will do it all themselves. Tell NORTHS that there will be awards to recognize those who produce the most in the least amount of time, and there is no doubt they will be first to receive top honors.

What "Turns On" NORTHS

- Action
- Challenge
- Goals
- Competition
- Negotiating
- Status
- Speed
- Winning

- Staying busy
- Making decisions
- Public recognition
- Independence
- Chances to shine
- Power and control
- Having authority
- Leadership roles

- Being the best
- Deadlines
- Responsibility
- Important tasks
- Practicality
- Productivity
- Taking charge
- Hard work

Disclosing NORTH Pet Peeves

NORTHS are irritated by anything which they perceive as wasting their time. They have little tolerance for long, repetitive discussions, particularly when firm decisions are not reached so that tasks can get underway immediately. It is best not to mention anything to NORTHS which can't or won't take place until well into the future, because they will become frustrated if they can't start on it right away. Plan ahead what you want to communicate to NORTHS, and say it as briefly and to-the-point as possible. Never tell NORTHS more than they actually need or want to know – it drives them crazy to have to weed through irrelevant details to get to the bottom line of any message.

What "Turns Off" NORTHS

- Indecision
- Beating around the bush
- Chit-chat
- Dependency
- Easily hurt feelings
- Irrelevant information
- Having little to do
- Having to follow orders
- Close supervision
- Insignificant busy work
- Slow pace
- Excuses
- Irresponsibility
- Lack of initiative
- Apathy
- Long explanations
- Procrastination
- Red tape
- Roadblocks to goals
- Self-pity

Igniting NORTHS

NORTHS Are Excited By . . .

- Important goals that must be met by a deadline
- Enough work to keep them challenged and busy
- Authority to negotiate and make some decisions
- Independence, without others "on their back"
- Leadership roles, formal or informal
- Opportunities to achieve higher status
- Public recognition for their accomplishments
- Productivity and initiative in others
- Competition, real or imagined
- Tough assignments

NORTHS Love To . . .

- Call the shots to meet goals
- Solve situational problems
- Work without a lot of assistance
- Make decisions that save time
- Handle impossible pressures
- Meet critical deadlines
- Compete to win or to get needed results
- Get right to the bottom line
- Establish purposeful parameters
- Negotiate conditions

Rewarding NORTHS

Listed below are a variety of things that NORTHS find rewarding. They can be used at home or at work as reinforcers to strengthen NORTH performances.

- Overt praise
- Choice of tasks or activities
- Increased responsibility and power
- Opportunities to make decisions that affect them
- Leadership roles
- Receiving compliments
- Quick follow-up on requests/questions
- Name on bulletin board for meeting a goal
- Positive comments on performance improvements
- Removal from constant supervision
- Award or plaque with their name on it
- Putting positive information into personal file
- Letting them report to persons of status
- Letter of commendation
- Memo to superiors about their achievement
- Training for better jobs
- Promotions to higher rank
- Raises based on merit
- Bonuses based on winning competitions
- Fringe benefits

Cushioning Clashes with NORTHS

A clash occurs when people, ideas or things which are different make contact and create friction or conflict. The greater the difference, the greater is the conflict. Many clashes among people are caused by differences in priorities. Remember:

- GOALS are naturally important to NORTHS
- FACTS are naturally important to EASTS
- VALUES are naturally important to SOUTHS
- METHODS are naturally important to WESTS

People clash most often over that which is naturally most important to them. Two or more NORTHS might clash over differing goals. NORTHS and EASTS might clash when goals conflict with facts. NORTHS and SOUTHS might clash when goals conflict with values, and NORTHS and WESTS might clash when goals conflict with methods.

Natural Clashes Between Opposites

NORTHS	vs	SOUTHS
Task-centered	vs	People-centered
Hardworking	vs	Laid-back
Independent	vs	Team players
Practical	vs	Emotional
Authoritarian leaders	vs	Democratic leaders
Business-like	vs	Personable
Controlling	vs	Helpful
Fast-paced	vs	Slow-paced

How to Avoid Conflict with NORTHS

- Focus on them
- Don't bother them
- Do it now
- Stay impersonal
- Let them lead
- Value their time
- Work fast and hard
- Respect their authority
- Give them the bottom line
- Don't complain
- Do what you promise

- Solve your own problems
- Think fast
- Try hard
- Meet deadlines
- Don't panic
- Remember what they say
- Stay busy
- Provide choices
- Be decisive
- Have goals

- Be realistic
- Stick to business
- Get to the point
- Help them look good
- Show independence
- Avoid excuses
- Take initiative
- Think of work as fun
- Be brief
- Ask their opinion
- Exhibit confidence

Do's and Don'ts of Living or Working with NORTHS

Do's

- Do – be sensitive to the NORTH ego
- Do – appreciate the NORTH sense of pride
- Do – help NORTHS feel important
- Do – compliment NORTHS when appropriate
- Do – recognize NORTHS' accomplishments
- Do – insist that NORTHS treat you with respect
- Do – give NORTHS guidelines, not orders
- Do – stand up to NORTHS when necessary
- Do – give NORTHS straight answers
- Do – keep up with NORTHS' fast pace

Give NORTHS What They Need

Although she had been warned that it was impossible to work with the new boss, Marlene got along fine with her. In fact, she got a promotion ahead of the other girls. Marlene listened to what she was told, and did it without argument as quickly as possible. She showed respect for her boss's authority, was honest and to the point when questioned by her, and praised her leadership. Once she realized that her boss was an ordinary person, too, just trying to do her job, it was easier to relax around her without feeling intimidated.

Don'ts

- Don't – let NORTHS intimidate you
- Don't – expect long conversations from NORTHS
- Don't – be overly sensitive to NORTH abruptness
- Don't – allow NORTHS to belittle you
- Don't – openly defy NORTHS
- Don't – complain or whine around NORTHS
- Don't – show cowardice or flagrant weakness
- Don't – fight with NORTHS – walk away until later
- Don't – dawdle and waste NORTHS' time
- Don't – ask NORTHS a lot of time-consuming questions

Don't Be Intimidated by Fear of a Blast

For years Francine had been afraid to stand up to her husband, Jake. As a result, their relationship was not close because she found herself avoiding him and "walking on eggshells" when she was with him. She hated herself for being weak and cowardly in his presence, but she didn't know how to change. One day, when Jake spoke to her as if she were a child, she somehow found the courage to confront him calmly. Looking him in the eye, she said, "Jake, please don't speak to me that way again. I am a grown woman and I do not deserve to be treated like a child." From that moment on, she felt stronger and began to assert her opinions in a non-threatening way. Jake responded by respecting her new-found courage and strength. Their marriage has never been stronger.

"Best Bets" for Compatibility with NORTHS

Take note spouses, children, friends, bosses and co-workers of NORTHs! A quick compatibility check will help you identify those who tend to get along best with NORTH people.

Personality types that are adjacent to NORTH on the Personality Compass (EAST and WEST) are naturally most compatible with NORTHS.

The highest degree of compatibility usually occurs when both the dominant and subdominant natures are adjacent on the Compass, as illustrated below.

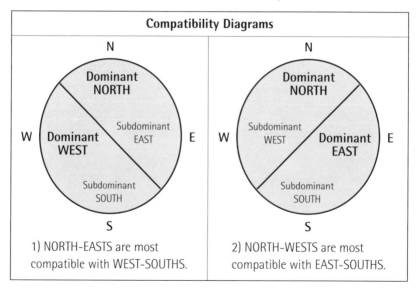

Compatibility Diagrams

1) NORTH-EASTS are most compatible with WEST-SOUTHS.

2) NORTH-WESTS are most compatible with EAST-SOUTHS.

"Cash In" on Compatibility with NORTHS

1) NORTH-EASTS and WEST-SOUTHS complement each other by completing the circle of qualities and talents that create well-rounded individuals and teams.

2) NORTH-WESTS and EAST-SOUTHS also function together productively because their natures are different, but not opposite, so they enrich each other.

NORTHS are not generally compatible with dominant SOUTHS because they are opposite in nature and have very little in common, unless both types are very well-rounded individuals.

NORTHS are not usually compatible with other dominant NORTHS because they both want control, but they do tend to respect other NORTHS. NORTHS need other types to help them achieve their fullest potential.

Tips for NORTHS to Get Along with Others

Directions: NORTHS, cross (X) off as you conquer each skill.

- [ ] Help people more often
- [ ] Think before you speak
- [ ] Go out of your way to be friendly
- [ ] Listen to others attentively
- [ ] Pay attention to the needs of others
- [ ] Try not to dominate
- [ ] Ask for others' opinions, ideas and feedback
- [ ] Share power by delegating responsibilities
- [ ] Value process, as well as bottom-line results
- [ ] Use diplomacy when dealing with people
- [ ] Slow down to avoid errors and stress
- [ ] Realize that teamwork accomplishes more
- [ ] Brainstorm for options before charging ahead
- [ ] Don't shout when you feel angry
- [ ] Develop patience and understanding
- [ ] Be less judgmental of others
- [ ] Become more humble
- [ ] Enjoy the game, not just the victory

- [ ] Broaden your perspectives
- [ ] Take a back seat for a while and relax
- [ ] Learn from constructive criticism
- [ ] Smell the flowers periodically
- [ ] Don't rush, and value others who take their time
- [ ] Make an effort not to hurt people's feelings
- [ ] Don't let little things make you irritable
- [ ] Make time for personal conversations and relationships
  - [ ] Be open-minded to other views
  - [ ] Develop more creativity
  - [ ] Give credit where credit is due
  - [ ] Enjoy people, not just work
  - [ ] Control your natural impatience
  - [ ] Empower others
  - [ ] Volunteer your service
  - [ ] Value kindness and gentleness

NORTHS, Beware!

When something upsets you, and you begin to feel justified in expressing your feelings by shouting or winning a physical match, STOP! Many NORTHS actually take pride in exhibiting a show of power, but you are probably the only person in the situation who shares the view. That behavior generally is not effective, and you may regret it later.

Targeting NORTHS for the Right Job

Terrific Jobs for NORTHS

- Chief Executive
- President
- Director
- Manager
- Foreman
- Supervisor
- Military Officer
- Project Leader
- Negotiator

- Headhunter
- Booking Agent
- Security Guard
- Chairperson
- Police Officer
- Maitre d'
- Conductor
- Coach
- Pilot

Memory Jogger

You need NORTHS on the job when . . .
- You need someone who can take charge and set goals
- You need a lot of tasks to be finished fast
- You need to complete a project by a deadline
- You need a person to "lay down the law"
- You need to confront people who owe you money

Fine-Tuning for NORTH Jobs

Jerry is a dominant NORTH-subdominant EAST nature. He is the perfect Manager of Shipping and Receiving because he likes to be in charge, meets every deadline and keeps perfect, detailed records.

James is a dominant NORTH-subdominant WEST nature. He is the perfect Chief Executive because he is assertive, makes quick decisions, and has the vision and risk-taking qualities to take the company where he wants it to go in the next ten years.

5 Jobs for NORTH–EAST People (and why)
1 Military Officer – leader (N), structured regulations (E)
2 Negotiator – assertive (N), analytical (E)
3 Chairperson – authoritative (N), organized (E)
4 Maitre d' – decisive (N), proper protocol (E)
5 Conductor – goal-centered (N), focused (E)

5 Jobs for NORTH–WEST People (and why)
1 Chief Executive – in control (N), visionary (W)
2 Manager – hardworking (N), flexible (W)
3 Project Leader – fast-paced deadlines (N), innovative (W)
4 Police Officer – fearless (N), risk taker (W)
5 Coach – action-centered (N), adaptable (W)

Why NORTHS Make Great Employees

NORTHS can be counted on to meet difficult challenges, even under extreme pressures. They are competitive and will do their best to achieve a goal and win, and they will do it faster than most by sticking to the basics for bottom-line results. The following examples illustrate NORTHS at their best.

NORTHS Can Take on a Challenge

Bryan, a NORTH Product Manager, was determined to increase the productivity of his department by 10 per cent over the previous year. He shared his goal with all of his department employees and created weekly competitions designed to help meet the challenge. He found ways to cut through time-consuming steps and still meet the quality control standards. After achieving the goal, one of his workers said of him, "He rolled up his sleeves and got in there with us on several occasions when the deadlines seemed impossible – but we did it! We produced 10 per cent more and got it out the door 10 per cent faster than we did last year, thanks to Bryan, who wouldn't let us give up or fail."

NORTHS Love to Win

Margaret, a NORTH Administrative Assistant, set up a competition between the secretaries in three different departments, offering individual plaques and a dinner at the city's finest restaurant as the reward for the victorious department. It is not surprising that her criteria for winning were based on turning in the departmental reports by the earliest deadline for three consecutive months, and increasing their combined departmental typing speed by the largest percentage over the same three-month period. Margaret's goal was increased speed and productivity within every department, and she achieved it.

NORTHS Hate to Waste Time

Gloria, a NORTH head nurse at a large hospital, sent the following memo to her floor nurses.

"Effective today, the following improvements are necessary to save time and increase productivity:

- Work faster. Spend less time talking with patients; do only what must be done and go directly to your next patient.

- Don't refer so many questions to me. Think first, and then make your own decisions whenever possible; you are all trained nurses, after all.

- Shorten your reports. Don't take a paragraph to say what you can say in a sentence."

NORTHS Can Take the Heat

Frank desperately needed to hire someone to replace Stan as Project Manager for the oil rig construction off the coast of Texas. It was way behind schedule, and meeting the August first deadline was critical because the hurricane season would soon follow. What Frank needed, he knew, was a NORTH-natured person because only a NORTH would be willing to take the heat for someone else's mistakes and still successfully bring the project in on time.

Top 3 Interview Questions & Answers That Help Hire NORTHS for NORTH Jobs

1 "Tell me about yourself."

NORTHS generally like to talk about their successes, so they might mention such things as:

- Outstanding work they have done
- Significant goals they have achieved
- Difficult tasks they have accomplished
- Leadership roles they have assumed
- Courageous battles they have fought
- Competitions they have won
- Titles they have held
- Awards they have received

2 "What interested you in our company (or the job in question)?"

NORTH interest is often whetted by:

- Important status
- Competitive challenge
- A great deal of action
- Exciting work to keep them busy
- Opportunities for growth and promotion
- Authority to make decisions and have some control
- Visible reward systems that recognize hard work
- Highly respected personnel

3 "Why *should* we hire you?"

NORTHS will often describe their own professional strengths as:

- Enjoying hard work
- Putting in long hours
- Seeing what needs to be done and doing it
- Getting tasks done fast
- Meeting goals
- Having the determination to overcome obstacles
- Completing projects ahead of schedule
- Handling pressure well

Famous NORTHS

(Based on historical perception)

Cleopatra
(Egocentric)

Winston Churchill
(Fearless)

Napoleon Bonaparte
(Forceful)

Evita Peron
(Ambitious)

Queen Victoria
(Assertive)

Mao Tse Tung
(Authoritative)

Henry Ford
(Goal-centered)

Ghengis Khan
(Courageous)

Implementing The Personality Compass:
If You Are a NORTH
(Dominant or Subdominant)

What Is Implementation?

Implementation is simply "putting into action", or using something for a particular purpose. *The Personality Compass* is a resource that simplifies the complexities of human behavior so that you can more easily understand yourself and the people around you. *The Personality Compass* also provides practical implementation exercises for you to use on a daily basis to help you develop and improve the entire gamut of personality traits and aptitudes. You can use this handbook for three very specific and useful purposes.

Use *The Personality Compass* to Achieve Results

● Develop a well-rounded balance of qualities and skills in yourself and increase your own self-esteem.

● Become an astute, other-oriented communicator and enrich all of your personal and professional relationships.

● Enhance both the breadth and depth of your competencies and increase your success on the job and in your daily life.

Using the Compass to Improve NORTHS

What To Do If You Are a NORTH

NORTHS must learn to think and act SOUTH:
- To achieve well-rounded balance
- When communicating with SOUTHS
- In situations, jobs or tasks that require SOUTH attributes and skills

Know what's in it for NORTHS to think and act SOUTH:
- You will improve your effectiveness in dealing with people
- You will become more likable and popular
- You will increase your ability to be well-rounded
- You will learn to value and develop your weaknesses
- You will get out of your comfort zone and grow
- You will develop self-esteem and power by accomplishing more

Think about the core of the SOUTH nature:
- SOUTHS have a peaceful and generous nature
- SOUTHS are unselfish and other-oriented
- SOUTHS genuinely listen and care about helping people
- SOUTHS love to please and make others happy
- SOUTHS avoid conflict and seek approval
- SOUTHS like to be part of a cooperative team
- SOUTHS can't rush themselves or others

Tips for NORTHS on How to Act More SOUTH

Step 1   Study the SOUTH sections and Chapter Five of this book.

Step 2   Think of SOUTHS you know, and ask yourself what they might say or do.

Step 3   Make a concentrated effort to think and act as if you are a dominant SOUTH.

Step 4   Force yourself to view the world and the people you meet from a SOUTH perspective.

Step 5   Practice! Practice! Practice! SOUTH behavior and skills can be learned.

Step 6   Start simply, using the following specific guidelines.

How to Act SOUTH Step-by-Step

Directions: place a cross (X) in the blank(s) you need to strengthen, then practice.

- ☐ Smile warmly and look into people's eyes
- ☐ Pause. Take time to socialize and chat with people
- ☐ Ask "How are you?" and listen actively to the response
- ☐ Avoid looking at your watch or around the room when talking
- ☐ Pitch in and help, no matter how busy you are
- ☐ Say a few sincere, kind words to the person you're with
- ☐ Stay off the subject of yourself and focus on others
- ☐ Bite your tongue to prevent yourself from arguing or shouting
- ☐ Hold on tightly to your chair when you want to take over
- ☐ Speak less, and speak softly when you do have something to say
- ☐ Make yourself slow down and stay patient and calm
- ☐ Count to ten when you feel like bragging or showing off
- ☐ Tune in to the way people feel, and the effects of your behavior on others
- ☐ Think about ways you can help someone
- ☐ Spend more time with family and friends

Specify What You Need

Evaluation Chart for NORTHS

Using the preceding pages as guidelines, list below the behaviors you need to develop first.

Example: _Listening skills_

- _____
- _____

- _____
- _____
- _____

List below a strategy to achieve each of the above.

Example: _Make sure I allow others to have their say_

- _____
- _____
- _____
- _____

Identify a SOUTH person you admire and four characteristics they have that you want/need. Name _____

- _____
- _____

- _____
- _____

Become What You Are Not

Chart For NORTHS to Track Your Progress

Directions: Track your behavior improvements in the chart below. Use a cross (X) to indicate status.

Behaviors I have strengthened	Improved in one week	Improved in one month
Watched typical SOUTHS	☐	☐
Smiled sincerely	☐	☐
Talked less	☐	☐
Asked about others' family	☐	☐
Developed compassion	☐	☐
Said thank you	☐	☐
Expressed feelings	☐	☐
Complimented others	☐	☐
Shared personal time	☐	☐
Felt more humble	☐	☐
Volunteered to help	☐	☐
Enjoyed people more	☐	☐
Put others first	☐	☐
Took more breaks	☐	☐
Didn't take over	☐	☐
Showed sincere affection	☐	☐

Behaviors I have strengthened	Improved in one week	Improved in one month
Gave a gift for no reason	☐	☐
Empowered others	☐	☐
Worked on teams	☐	☐
Stopped shouting	☐	☐
Put people above tasks	☐	☐
Showed more vulnerability	☐	☐
Cooperated with others	☐	☐

Resources I have implemented	Implemented in one week	Implemented in one month
Mentored with a SOUTH	☐	☐
Read about SOUTHS	☐	☐
Observed many SOUTHS	☐	☐
Learned to value SOUTHS	☐	☐
Practiced being SOUTH	☐	☐

Using the Personality Compass to Improve NORTH Relationships

Understanding the NORTH "Blind Spot"

Stand in one place and hold your head perfectly still, facing straight ahead. Roll your eyes as far to the left and right as possible, and note exactly what lies within your realm of vision. That which lies just beyond what you can see in your peripheral vision is known as your "blind spot". It is there, but you simply can't see it.

Human nature also has "blind spots". You can see things in others that they do not see in themselves – and others can see things in you that you have trouble seeing in yourself. The most common "blind spot" in NORTHS, which can cause problems for themselves and others, is putting work as a top priority. They don't perceive themselves as task-driven, yet it is at the core of their nature.

NORTH Drive Can Hurt Relationships

More than once Gabe found himself surprised at being accused of not caring for his family. How could his wife, Ellie, say that? Of course he loved them. If he didn't, why would he work twelve to fifteen-hour days to give them the lifestyle they could now enjoy? He spent his entire life working long, hard hours to build a successful business so that his family could have the best of everything. How could his wife be so ungrateful? And how could she say he didn't know her or the children? They just had a terrific trip to Europe together. It would have been silly to waste that opportunity to clinch some foreign business markets while he was there, and after all, he managed to join them for some wonderful gourmet meals at dinner. What does she mean "she needs more"? She has everything any woman could want.

Perception: The Root of Most Problems

Ellie's perception

- Ellie loves Gabe and their children, and needs to spend more time with them all together as a family unit.

- Ellie respects Gabe's need to work hard, but not when it interferes with time that has been set aside for the family to enjoy precious moments together.

- Ellie needs to know that Gabe loves her and the children enough to make certain sacrifices and give them his undivided attention on special occasions.

Gabe's perception

- Gabe loves Ellie and their children, and wants to work hard to give them the best of everything.

- Gabe respects Ellie's need for family time, but not when it forces him to disregard practical opportunities that would be very costly to pursue at another time.

- Gabe needs to feel that love will not force him into a corner so exclusive that there is no room for other things that could be important to him or critical to the family's future.

Solutions: Give and Take

- Compromise is at the heart of any solution to a problem.

- Ellie and Gabe need to communicate about their feelings and needs, and negotiate what each is willing to accept from the other.

- Ellie should gently reveal how Gabe's "workaholic" task centeredness affects the family.

- Gabe needs to set aside and honor more time spent with his wife and family each week. He should allow only emergencies or truly critical issues to interfere with that allotted time.

- Ellie needs to accept the agreed upon time which Gabe spends with her and the family, without always wanting more. When extenuating circumstances do arise, she should accept them graciously, so long as they do not revert to the rule, rather than the exception.

Questions & Answers About the NORTH Personality

Question   Why do some NORTHS get upset when a person dares to disagree with them, or when their actions are questioned, or when someone refuses to do what they tell them to do?

Answer   *To a NORTH nature that is innately fast-paced and goal-centered, these issues are rooted mostly in NORTH efforts to get a job completed as quickly as possible. In the NORTH brain, they are usually confident of being right, and often perceive disagreement, questioning and rebellion against their authority as roadblocks to successfully achieving their goal(s). In NORTH reasoning, it simply makes sense to follow them without question because they have the confidence to truly believe they know best, not only for themselves, but for everyone. They are not comfortable with democratic discussions that require a vote or slow down the tasks they deem important. Keep in mind that NORTHS can't really help their nature – but they can and should learn to "go SOUTH" when these characteristics prevent them from listening and considering the ideas and needs of others.*

Question   Why do some NORTHS have a way of making others feel intimidated and fearful – that if people don't meet with their approval they will somehow get in trouble, or lose the relationship forever?

Answer   *Most NORTHS don't mean to make people feel afraid, nor do they intentionally threaten one's sense of security. Because their assertive nature focuses on the fastest, surest way to achieve success, and their brain rushes headlong toward action without hesitation, most NORTHS actually believe they are being helpful when they offer their unsolicited advice on what to do and how to do it for faster results. However, that information can be quite painful or infuriating to a non-NORTH who doesn't perceive their message in that light.*

Question **Why do some NORTHS seem to enjoy being rude and unpleasant to others with no sense of embarrassment about their insensitive behavior?**

Answer *Because NORTHS by nature value power, strength and getting a job done fast, they may perceive people who are not similar to them as weak or incompetent, and therefore feel they are deserving of their wrath. In their belief that they are justified in their judgment, they may also feel justified to "set those people straight" by telling them off. Their own stress or exhaustion level, as well as their own sense of self-esteem, frequently play major roles in how they treat others. An important lesson for NORTHS to learn is that people learn far better from respectful and effective communication than from painfully inflicted accusations or tirades.*

Chapter Four

Valuing the Nature
of EAST

The Uniqueness of EAST

Typical EAST
- Quality-centered
- Detailed, structured
- Slow, deliberate
- Focused, tenacious
- Organized planner
- Logical, analytical
- Proper, punctual
- Industrious, responsible
- Traditional, conservative
- Serious, reserved

Extreme EAST
- Perfectionist
- Humorless, inflexible
- Bogged down
- Obsessive, oblivious
- Tunnel-visioned, habitual
- Critical, ritualistic
- Nagging, unforgiving
- Unrelenting, stubborn
- Isolated loner
- Narrowminded

EASTS at a Glance

"EASTS Do It with Class"

- **Motto** EASTS do it right the first time
- **Symbol** Planetary orbit
- **Greatest strength** Planning in detail
- **Basic weakness** Tunnel vision
- **Fundamental aptitude** Logical analysis
- **Priority** Facts
- **Motivational turn-on** Looking for errors
- **Pet peeve** Inaccuracy
- **Work and play style** Serious
- **Main work competency** Organization
- **Pace** Slow and cautious
- **Image** Quality

EAST Role Model

It is said that Benjamin Franklin was searching for an editor to help run his newspaper. Franklin invited one applicant out to lunch, and later politely informed him that the job was wrong for him. When the applicant asked why, Franklin answered that it was because the applicant salted his steak before tasting it. He said that the job required an individual who would never jump to conclusions or make assumptions.

Top 10 Super Strengths of EASTS

Typical EASTS might often exhibit:

1 Analysis
2 Organization
3 Industriousness
4 Concentration
5 Focus
6 Tenacity
7 Logic
8 Insight
9 Propriety
10 Responsibility

EASTS Can Take Monotony

Ann did so well in her job on the assembly line at a major motor company in Detroit that she was promoted to a managerial position. After only three months in her new job, Anna requested to be returned to her job on the line because, as she put it, "I knew exactly what was expected every day, and I knew instantly if I did my job perfectly or not – it was black or white, right or wrong, and I loved doing the same thing, the same way. It was clear and unconfusing." Routine and monotony are comfortable for EASTS.

From Super Strengths to Team Stars

How EASTS Charge-Up a Team

Most EASTS naturally help the teams they are on by:

- Building team quality and excellence
- Motivating team players to perfect their skills
- Raising individual and team competence levels
- Increasing team efficiency
- Developing a team game plan
- Turning individual diversity into team precision
- Keeping each player disciplined for reaching the team goal
- Instilling team strategies to excel
- Inspiring their team to organize ways to achieve success
- Planning/practicing their team to victory

When EAST Team Leadership Works Best

The EAST tight-rein leadership style is most effective when:

- dependent or inexperienced individuals or teams need to believe they know what to do and are in control, even if they are being led behind the scenes;
- hostile or out-of-control individuals or teams need someone to maintain order and protect them from themselves or others, while not antagonizing their need to feel they have legitimate authority or power.

Top 10 Danger Zones of EASTS

Extreme EASTS might often exhibit:

1 Obsession
2 Pessimism
3 Over-caution
4 Criticism
5 Tedium
6 Sarcasm
7 Narrowmindedness
8 Isolation
9 Argumentation
10 Snobbishness

EASTS Can Take Perfectionism Too Far

On a bad day, Pete, an EAST foreman of the machine shop, does not tolerate tardiness, dirty machines, rubble in the aisles, substandard workmanship or dawdling among machinists. Every station has charts posted that specify exact hours worked, process flow details, data inventories, quality control specifications, performance measurements, communication systems, and triple check lists to ensure zero defects. When one of his machinists quit because of the stress created by Pete's impossible standards, he left a large sign posted on Pete's door that read, "Get a life!"

From Danger Zones to Dynamite

- EAST *pessimism* and *overcautiousness* can sometimes result in sound decision-making and improved safety.

  When someone tends to take wild risks, or when someone overlooks potentially hazardous situations or equipment, EASTS can point them out and give precise reasons for their perceptions.

- EAST *obsessiveness* and *tediousness* can sometimes result in finding "the needle in the haystack".

  When facts or errors are lost in mountains of data or chaos, EASTS can have the patience and tenacity to dig through the details to find exactly what they are looking for.

- EAST *narrowmindedness* and *argumentativeness* can sometimes result in effective negotiation.

  When in the midst of contract negotiations, EASTS can focus everyone on their particular issues until they can prove their point logically and convince others of their position.

- EAST *criticism* and *sarcasm* can sometimes result in improved quality and efficiency.

  When someone is not meeting the required standards of workmanship or productivity, EASTS can sometimes shame them into improving.

- EAST *isolation* and *snobbishness* can sometimes result in independent thinking and decisions when that is needed.

  On juries, and in meetings where it is important to be able to make fair or profitable decisions based on facts alone, EASTS can stand alone on evidence and justify their principles.

Understanding the Differences Between EAST-NORTHS and EAST-SOUTHS

Recognizing and remembering the natural strengths and abilities of people within the north, east, south and west compass directions is easy because *The Personality Compass* shows the similarities between North, East, South and West cultures and the four cultural natures. We know that EAST people have characteristics that are similar to those found in Eastern cultures, but we can know even more about them if we can also identify their subdominant nature, which is adjacent on the compass.

Sarah and Mark: Alike and Different

Sarah has most of her qualities in common with East cultures, and, because she is a dominant EAST-subdominant NORTH, she has a high number of qualities in common with North cultures. Mark, a dominant EAST – subdominant SOUTH, shares much in common with Sarah because of their similar EAST qualities, but because of their opposite subdominant natures, Sarah and Mark are different in many ways.

A significant impact on the types of tasks that appeal to an individual, as well as on the aptitudes required to achieve quality and excellence at the tasks, is made by both the dominant and subdominant natures. An EAST-NORTH, Sarah is structured, detailed, assertive, decisive and fast-paced. Mark, as an EAST–SOUTH, is structured, detailed, friendly, helpful and slow-paced. Even though both are dominant EASTS, they would have differing interests and talents, and would not be equally suited to the same job.

EAST-NORTH People

Structured • Detailed • Assertive • Decisive • Fast-Paced

EAST-SOUTH People

Structured • Detailed • Friendly • Helpful • Slow-paced

Recognizing EAST Behaviors

Twenty or more crosses (X) *indicate a strong EAST nature.*

EASTS in general . . .

- ☐ Have excellent, erect posture
- ☐ Appear thoughtful and serious
- ☐ Are punctual, or early
- ☐ Wear tasteful, conservative clothing
- ☐ Take precise, almost measured steps
- ☐ Exhibit an intellectual demeanor
- ☐ Seem reserved and somewhat aloof
- ☐ Keep their emotions under control
- ☐ Sound knowledgeable and articulate
- ☐ Give accurate, exact information
- ☐ Argue because they enjoy persuasion
- ☐ Think logically, in terms of cause and effect
- ☐ Do one thing at a time, in structured sequence
- ☐ Follow exact directions / instructions

- [ ] Think before they speak or act
- [ ] Can sit still for long periods of time
- [ ] Speak slowly and carefully
- [ ] Work on a project until it is finished
- [ ] Evade personal questions
- [ ] Provide precise details
- [ ] Make decisions only after careful evaluation
- [ ] Hate disorganization and sloppiness
- [ ] Appreciate manners and proper etiquette
- [ ] Display strong concentration and focus
- [ ] Insist on doing tasks right the first time
- [ ] Become angry over errors or poor quality
- [ ] Confront conflicts from an analytical approach
- [ ] Talk, move and eat with slow deliberateness
- [ ] Leave no stone unturned to find the right answer
- [ ] Find incompetence intolerable
- [ ] Put facts as a top priority
- [ ] Can be critical of non-EASTS
- [ ] Like to follow the rules
- [ ] Value quality, logic and accuracy

CAUTION

Recognizing EAST Children

Typical EAST Children in General . . .
- Care about their appearance
- Avoid getting terribly dirty or messy
- Get into planned routines easily
- Ask "why?" often and expect correct answers
- Prefer mental games to physical games
- Focus on one toy or project for a long time
- Take things apart and put them together
- Put themselves on a schedule
- Try hard to follow the rules and do what is proper
- Like the structure of school, and like to learn

Erica seemed to be borne on a schedule. You could set your watch by the precise hour she would get hungry, fall asleep and wake up. By the time she was two years old, Erica had a definite idea about what she wanted to wear – and every outfit had to match and be color coordinated. At the age of ten she won a prize for building the most perfect, detailed sandcastle on the beach. Her teachers loved her because learning excited her, and because her papers were always neat, turned in on time, and she never failed to follow instructions exactly.

Extreme EAST Children in General . . .
- Are under some degree of stress
- May change clothes several times a day
- Can be obsessive about what belongs to them
- Get very upset if a toy gets broken
- Insist on a special place for everything
- Worry about things that might happen
- Dislike their personal space being invaded
- Become intolerant of deviation from rules/routine
- Will sit for hours without physical exercise
- Hate being teased or joking around

Kelsey pouted and refused to eat every time her grandmother put food on her plate, much to the dismay of her loving Nanny, who was only trying to be helpful. The fact was, Kelsey couldn't stand the thought of her peas mixing with her potatoes or meat or salad or bread. Not only that, she liked to eat her food in a certain order, clockwise, and that's how she wanted each item placed on her plate. She wished her grandmother would let her fix her own plate.

Recognizing EASTS in Different Roles

As Students
EASTS in General . . .

- Ask detailed questions
- Are quick to point out errors made by instructors
- Become upset when discussions get off track
- Have little tolerance for exaggeration and inaccuracy
- Enjoy mental challenges
- Turn in neat, nearly perfect papers
- Take education seriously
- Argue over logical points and minutiae
- Come across as studious and intellectual
- Like to analyze reasons for everything
- Often confirm assignments with teachers after class
- Pay careful attention and stay focused

As Athletes
EASTS in General . . .

- Are extremely disciplined
- Enjoy the routine of daily practice
- Work constantly toward perfecting their skills
- Will try over and over until they get it right
- Show up early and are always prepared
- May be the smartest, if not the strongest and fastest
- Need to know the reasons behind the game plan
- Expect schedules to be followed precisely
- May be critical of horseplay
- Worry about preparation/details
- Analyze and plan strategies to improve quality of play
- Focus on how to do better, even if they win

As Leaders
EASTS in General . . .

- Employ a tight-rein leadership style and may make covert decisions
- Are very well organized and require it of others
- Keep meticulous records
- Insist on following a strategic plan
- Make sure the budget is balanced and are conservative spenders
- Have a firm set of rules and regulations
- Follow policy to the letter
- Begin meetings and events on time
- Favor parliamentary procedure over casual structure
- Tolerate lengthy, detailed discussions
- Prefer to do tasks themselves, and do them "right"
- Like to do things the traditional way

As Friends, Spouses or Parents
EASTS in General . . .

- Have good manners and expect it in others
- Correct others with the words "you should"
- May have an air of mystery, aloofness
- Argue over trivialities
- Consider exaggerations and inaccuracies as lies
- Expect others to share their high standards
- Need cleanliness and organization
- Keep mental records of whose "turn" it is to do tasks
- Like equality in relationships
- Appreciate quality name brands
- Maintain structure and routine in their daily lives
- Are reliable, competent and offer a sense of security to others

Recognizing EASTS in Different Situations

At Home
EASTS in General . . .

- Provide a sense of order and consistency
- Like everything kept in its proper place
- Keep a meticulous home and grounds
- Are reserved in display of emotions
- Enjoy privacy (may put up fences)
- Drive quality vehicles that are efficient
- Maintain long and detailed "To Do" lists
- Rely on a daily planner and calendar
- Try to reason with their children
- Tidy up incessantly
- Get upset over unannounced visitors
- Live by a daily routine

In a Social Environment
EASTS in General . . .

- Sit back and observe others (and may seem critical)
- Appear poised and polished
- Have impeccable manners and respect that in others
- Expect excellent service
- Enjoy and often provide stimulating conversation
- Avoid wild and crazy activities
- Will not risk making fools of themselves
- May be considered "poor sports"
- Sometimes leave early
- Are picky about the invitations they accept
- Split shared bills exactly to the penny
- Prefer an evening at home alone to a party

During an Interview
EASTS in General . . .

- May arrive 15 minutes early
- Make good eye contact but avoid staring
- Shake hands properly, not too firmly
- Dress with conservative professionalism
- Display perfectly polished shoes, manicured nails
- Wait for an invitation to be seated
- Speak intelligently and may ask questions
- Are articulate and well-mannered
- Will probably have done their homework on the company
- Show concern for rules, procedures, systems
- Need to know exact expectations, facts
- Have their resume and references ready

On the Job
EASTS in General . . .

- Double and triple check their work
- Take their responsibility seriously
- Are slow because they are careful and cautious
- Become critical of shoddy workmanship in others
- Like work to be done correctly the first time
- May be picky about who they work with
- Focus and concentrate on one thing at a time
- Perform tasks in a logical, methodical sequence
- Finish what they start
- Can work well alone and in confined areas
- Enjoy detailed tasks that require accuracy
- Maintain organized space and records

Common Comments That Recognize Typical EASTS

"Marge is the perfect hostess. It must take her months to plan a party because every detail is in order, from th color coordinated lily pads floating in the pool to the engraved place cards and thematic menu and music selections."

Lori J.

"If you want to know every legal trick in the book to minimize your taxes, just call Lee. He has spent years developing his system into a science, and every deduction is safely within the law."

Preston F.

"We are so proud of our son, Andre. His voice coach at Julliard told us that he's never had a more technically disciplined student. In fact, he said that if Andre continues to focus on developing the emotional nuances of the music, he will no doubt make it to the Met!"

Robelard and Vivienne C.

Common Comments That Recognize Extreme EASTS

"*Louis drives me crazy. Every morning it feels as if someone winds him up and programmes him for the day. He never deviates from the same rigid routine. He opens the blinds, brushes his teeth, takes a shower, shaves, dresses, pours a cup of coffee, cuts a banana into his cereal, feeds the cat, eats a bowl of cereal, brushes his teeth again, grabs his briefcase and leaves the house. I can set my watch – the procedure takes 37 minutes, exactly.*"

Marian S.

"*Carol makes lists to remind her to look at her lists! Honestly, if she spent as much time doing as she did making lists of things to do, she wouldn't need a list!*"

Agnes R.

"*Ron gets so absorbed in his computer that he doesn't hear the telephone ring, he ignores the kids when they ask him for help with their homework, and he even forgets to eat. Is irreconcilable competition with a computer grounds for a divorce?*"

Heather E.

Motivating EASTS for Success

Tell EASTS that there is a mistake somewhere, and they will work non-stop until they find it. Tell them you admire and respect their competence and the consistent and excellent quality of their work, and they will achieve close to perfection. Tell them you need their plan, and EASTS will present you with every detail of how to master quality at the lowest price, using the most efficient methods, as well as structured, step-by-step, measures for implementing the plan. Tell EASTS that there will be an annual Quality Award presented to the employee who meets the highest standards of excellence throughout the year, and there is no doubt they will produce superior work that will exceed expectations.

What "Turns On" EASTS

- Quality
- Accurate records
- Looking for errors
- Competent workers
- Proving a point
- Structure
- Good manners
- Organization

- Planning in detail
- Not being rushed
- Traditional methods
- Serious work
- Meeting requirements
- Following rules
- Clear expectations
- Ideal work conditions

- Logical analysis
- Focusing on facts
- Quiet isolation
- Measurement tools
- Schedules
- Aim for perfection
- Efficiency
- Excellence

Disclosing EAST Pet Peeves

EASTS are turned off by anything which they perceive as poor quality or unreliable information. They have little tolerance for mediocrity or incompetence, particularly when either can cost in quality, efficiency or profit dollars. It is best not to wait until the last minute to give EASTS anything, because they require time to ponder and plan prior to taking action. Get your facts and details straight before you talk to EASTS, and give them information in a logical, step-by-step way. Never omit even one detail or step that EASTS consider important, or it can topple your credibility with them almost immediately – and it may take a long time for them to be able to trust you again. EASTS can make invaluable contributions so long as they are not immobilized by frustration.

What "Turns Off" EASTS

- Low standards
- Change
- Disregard for quality
- Ambiguous procedures
- Vague answers to questions
- Inaccurate information
- Roadblocks to facts/truth
- Costly shortcuts
- Imprecise record-keeping
- Self-indulgence
- Being rushed
- Chaos/noise
- Generalities
- Joking around
- Frivolous tasks
- Unreliability
- Incompetence
- Exaggeration
- Lack of focus
- Fast pace

Igniting EASTS

EASTS Are Excited By . . .

- Sequential tasks that can be done one at a time
- Sufficient time to finish what they start and check it
- Privacy, peace and quiet with few interruptions
- Opportunities to plan ahead in detail
- Editorial or inspection roles (to prevent errors)
- Authority to control quality of products or services
- Organized systems that assure accuracy and efficiency
- Consistency and competence in fellow-workers
- Excellence in everything
- Exceeding expected standards

EASTS Love To . . .

- Organize data, events
- Plan and double-check details and protocol
- Make quality inspections
- Provide accurate, factual reports
- Focus on instructions and follow exact rules
- Create and adhere to schedules
- Measure progress, efficiency, quality
- Analyze all options before making a decision
- Persuade through logical argumentation
- Live and work in a structured environment

Rewarding EASTS

Listed below are a variety of things that EASTS find rewarding. They can be used at home or at work as reinforcers to strengthen EAST performances.

- Praise in the presence of people they admire
- Gold or silver trophies or jewelry
- Blue ribbons
- Leather planner
- Meaningful books
- Historical documents or heirlooms
- Gourmet dinner for two
- Traditional art
- Conventional poetry
- Symphony or opera tickets
- A quiet, isolated environment for work
- Approval for their competence
- Awards for excellence
- Quality pen and pencil set
- Words that enhance their reputation
- Classic/quality name brand items
- Fine crystal or china pieces
- Engraved stationery
- Designer accessories
- Computer software that improves efficiency

Cushioning Clashes with EASTS

The greater the difference between people, ideas or things when they make contact and create friction, the greater is the conflict. Many clashes among people are caused by differences in priorities. Remember:

- GOALS are naturally important to NORTHS
- FACTS are naturally important to EASTS
- VALUES are naturally important to SOUTHS
- METHODS are naturally important to WESTS

People clash most often over that which is naturally most important to them. For example, two or more EASTS might clash over differing interpretations of the facts. EASTS and NORTHS might clash when facts conflict with goals. EASTS and SOUTHS might clash when facts conflict with values, and EASTS and WESTS might clash when facts conflict with methods.

Natural Clashes Between Opposites

EASTS	vs	WESTS
Fact-centered	v	Idea-centered
Traditional	v	Innovative
Structured	v	Changeable
Tight-rein leaders	v	Free-rein leaders
Conservative planners	v	Liberal risk-takers
Analytical pragmatists	v	Creative visionaries
Rule followers	v	Rule breakers
Slow-paced/sequential	v	Fast-paced/flexible

How to Avoid Conflict with EASTS

- Care about quality
- Don't leave messes
- Do it right
- Stay on track
- Focus on details
- Value their intelligence
- Work methodically
- Respect their routine
- Provide accurate information
- Don't exaggerate
- Do more than expected

- Finish what you start
- Think logically
- Follow directions
- Meet standards
- Don't skip steps
- Remember procedures
- Stay disciplined
- Give them time
- Be efficient
- Have a plan

- Be organized
- Get the facts straight
- Double-check for errors
- Provide proof
- Show tenacity
- Avoid mistakes
- Have good manners
- Aim for perfection
- Be analytical
- Ask why
- Exhibit competence

Do's and Don'ts of Living or Working with EASTS

Do's

- Do – be sensitive to the EAST need for structure
- Do – appreciate the EAST sense of propriety
- Do – help EASTS feel organized, focused
- Do – compliment EASTS' logical analysis
- Do – recognize EASTS' competence
- Do – insist that EASTS consider your opinion
- Do – give EASTS privacy, and don't rush them
- Do – stand up against EASTS' demands for perfection
- Do – give EASTS accurate, detailed answers
- Do – keep up with EASTS' quality standards

Give EASTS What They Need

Word was out that it was impossible to please Professor Yashimoto. Students who turned in papers the first week of classes with one misspelled word, or one fragment, or one run-on sentence were not happy about the big red Fs on their papers. They marched in droves to the Dean's office to complain that just because Yashimoto needed to nit-pick over every detail they shouldn't be penalized for his obsession with perfection. Yet, at the end of the semester, Dean Maxwell was amused when one of those students thanked the professor publicly during his graduation speech for demanding excellence and helping his students to expect it of themselves.

Don'ts

- Don't – let EASTS make you feel inferior
- Don't – expect a wild sense of humor from EASTS
- Don't – be overly sensitive to EAST criticism
- Don't – allow EASTS to set your personal standards
- Don't – openly contradict EASTS
- Don't – complain about cost of quality around EASTS
- Don't – show disregard for details
- Don't – fight with EASTS – use logical persuasion
- Don't – dawdle, but take the time to be careful
- Don't – ask why schedules must be followed

Don't be Intimidated by Fear of Not Measuring Up

Alex couldn't remember his father ever telling him, "Son, I'm really proud of you." It seemed that he was never quite smart enough, or clever enough, or fast enough, or disciplined enough, or ambitious enough to warrant his father's approval. At some point during his college years, Alex decided that he would do his personal best and stop measuring himself by his father's standards and expectations. Forty years later he was shocked as he sat by his father on the old man's death bed and finally heard the words he'd been longing to hear all his life: "Son," his father said, "I've always been proud of you. I criticized your weaknesses to help you grow, because your strengths were already perfect."

"Best Bets" for Compatibility with EASTS

Take note spouses, children, friends, bosses and co-workers of EASTS! A quick compatibility check will help you identify those who tend to get along best with EAST people.

Personality types that are adjacent to EAST on the Personality Compass (NORTH and SOUTH) are naturally most compatible with EASTS. The highest degree of compatibility usually occurs when both the dominant and subdominant natures are adjacent on the Compass, as illustrated below.

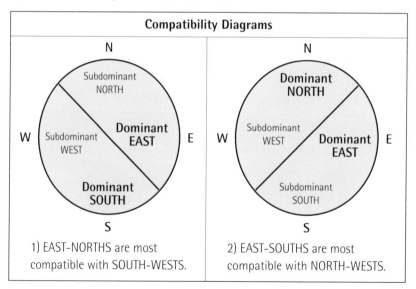

Compatibility Diagrams

1) EAST-NORTHS are most compatible with SOUTH-WESTS.

2) EAST-SOUTHS are most compatible with NORTH-WESTS.

"Cash In" on Compatibility with EASTS

1) EAST-NORTHS and SOUTH-WESTS complement each other by completing the circle of qualities and talents that create well-rounded individuals and teams.

2) EAST-SOUTHS and NORTH-WESTS also function together productively because their natures are different, but not opposite, so they enrich each other.

EASTS are not generally compatible with dominant WESTS because they are opposite in nature and have very little in common, unless both types are very well-rounded individuals.

EASTS are usually compatible with other dominant EASTS because they have similar interests and qualities, but they need other types to help them achieve their fullest potential.

Tips for EASTS to Get Along with Others

Directions: EASTS, cross (X) off as you conquer each skill.

- [ ] Loosen up a bit
- [ ] Get past the trees and see the forest
- [ ] Be more tolerant of innovative ideas
- [ ] Avoid being covert and secretive
- [ ] Be less critical of others
- [ ] Don't analyze things to death
- [ ] Enjoy the fun of change and spontaneity
- [ ] Resist the temptation to correct others publicly
- [ ] Realize that your debate may be perceived as arguing
- [ ] Allow people the luxury of human imperfections
- [ ] Let yourself look grubby for a change
- [ ] Realize that minute details can seem boring and unimportant
- [ ] Ask for help without feeling incompetent
- [ ] Try something different from time to time
- [ ] Express your feelings, not just logical opinions
- [ ] Let down your guard occasionally
- [ ] Don't worry so much
- [ ] Become more flexible

- [ ] Roll up your sleeves and get dirty
- [ ] Accept new ways of doing things
- [ ] Don't get bogged down in your own thoughts
- [ ] Resist turning your nose up at that which is not the very finest
- [ ] Have realistic expectations of yourself and others
- [ ] Forgive yourself and others for not being perfect
- [ ] Concentrate on not making others feel inferior
- [ ] Fight your tendency to have tunnel vision

                     - [ ] Practice wearing a warm smile
                     - [ ] Develop a sense of humor
                     - [ ] Don't take yourself so seriously
                     - [ ] See other perspectives
                     - [ ] Do things out of sequence when possible
                     - [ ] Permit yourself to be creative
                     - [ ] Get off "square one"
                     - [ ] Take a risk

EASTS, Beware!

When someone's lack of organization, tidiness, accuracy or quality frustrates you and you feel like nagging them, STOP! Many of you believe that you are helping people when you criticize others in an effort to improve their way of doing things, but that EAST behavior is almost never appreciated by anyone.

Targeting EASTS for the Right Job

Terrific Jobs for EASTS

- Judge
- Attorney
- Surgeon
- Engineer
- Editor
- Quality Control Inspector
- Researcher
- Accountant
- Investigator

- Data Processor/Programmer
- Finance Officer
- Military Strategist
- City Planner
- Efficiency Expert
- Statistician
- High-Tech Sales Rep
- Secretary
- Museum Curator

Memory Jogger

You need EASTS on the job when . . .

- You need detailed accuracy and/or top quality
- You need to prove a point in a logical, analytical way
- You need a person who will meet exact requirements
- You need to find errors or discover why something happened
- You need someone who can do tedious work for long hours alone

Fine-Tuning for EAST Jobs

Mel is a dominant EAST-subdominant NORTH nature. He is the perfect attorney because he likes to follow the letter of the law, he thinks and expresses himself logically and analytically, and he has the courage and confidence to perform well to an audience.

Laura is a dominant EAST-subdominant SOUTH nature. She is the perfect City Planner because she enjoys planning in detail, can use her computer skills for computer assisted design, and has the sensitivity to perceive what the people in cities of the future will need.

5 Jobs for EAST–NORTH People (and why)
1 Judge – structured (E), decisive (N)
2 Attorney – detailed (E), assertive (N)
3 Surgeon – focused (E), confident (N)
4 Engineer – analytical (E), determined (N)
5 Quality Control Inspector – quality-centered (E), takes initiative (N)

5 Jobs for EAST–SOUTH People (and why)
1 Editor – detailed (E), patient (S)
2 City Planner - plans well (E), process-centered (S)
3 High-Tech Sales Rep – punctual (E), friendly (S)
4 Secretary – proper protocol (E), helpful (S)
5 Museum Curator – responsible (E), slow-paced (S)

Why EASTS Make Great Employees

Trying to force EASTS to lower their standards, or prevent them from doing their very best at all times, would be a losing battle. Failing to use their thrifty, efficient nature and their ability to plan ahead in minute detail would be a mistake, because they can anticipate potential problems before they occur and set up systems that save important profit dollars. EASTS, as a rule, will not stay where there is gross inefficiency, shoddy workmanship or incompetence.

EASTS Can Take on a Debate

Julian listened to the other candidates and took mental notes on the fallacies he picked up in his opponents' reasoning. When it was his turn to speak, he blew their arguments apart with his incisive logic as he rebutted each point, step by step. Audience support was visibly shifted in his favor as Julian increased his credibility by presenting a convincing analysis and evidence for his position on each issue. At his victory party two weeks later, many voters said he changed their point of view as a result of the competence he displayed during the televised debate.

EASTS Love to Analyze

Walter, an EAST efficiency expert, traveled from plant to plant examining corporate systems for areas where there might be waste. His job was to find ways to improve efficiency that would result in reduced costs and higher overall profits for the company. He loved analyzing each department and focusing on what was not cost-efficient, and he could be absolutely objective when the time came to recommend cuts. Walter could logically analyze every possible option, and then make his decisions based only on the facts.

EASTS Hate to Make Mistakes

Karl, a scientific researcher for a major medical laboratory, kept the following checklist posted over his desk and followed the formula to the letter in an effort to minimize errors that would result in false data.

- Observe
- Test observations
- Record the results
- Test again
- Record the results
- Think about the results

- Draw conclusions from the results
- Analyze possible flaws in the conclusions
- Re-test for accuracy of conclusions
- Record provable conclusions

EASTS Can Take Responsibility

The Secretary to the Chief Executive was a tough position to fill. Dozens of men and women had applied, but Charles Carr knew that no one interviewed yet was the miracle worker he needed at his side to keep him organized, run the office to perfection, and be able to retrieve data he might need on a moment's notice. Then Tess appeared. When Charles was called away from the office during the interview for an emergency, Tess answered his telephone when no one else picked it up, took clear notes that included who called, the telephone number, and the purpose of the call. After 15 minutes elapsed, she stepped outside the office and asked the receptionist if it would be best for her to wait outside his office until he returned. Not only was she competent and efficient, but she respected proper protocol.

Top 3 Interview Questions & Answers That Help Hire EASTS for EAST Jobs

1 "Tell me about yourself."

EASTS generally like to talk about the quality of their work, so they might mention such things as:

- Measurable standards of excellence they have met or exceeded
- Detailed accounts of previous assignments
- Complicated or impressive details about their work
- Technological or other highly valuable skills they possess
- Quality functions, events or projects which they planned
- Efficiency improvement systems they have initiated
- Degrees or certifications which give them credibility
- Experts they know in their field

2 "What interested you in our company (or the job in question)?"

EAST interest is often whetted by:

- Quality products or services
- A structured, well-organized work environment
- Detailed work that requires precision
- Opportunities to prove their expertise
- Working with serious, competent people
- Efficient systems and policies
- Respectability and propriety
- Reputation for excellence and high standards

3 "Why *should* we hire you?"

EASTS will often describe their own professional strengths as:
- Meeting standards for excellence
- Checking for accuracy
- Being competent, industrious and reliable
- Having patience with tedious and repetitious tasks
- Thinking logically and analytically
- Following through to the very end
- Planning in minute detail and implementing the plan
- Performing quality work and always giving their best

Famous EASTS
(Based on historical perception)

Isaac Newton
(Analytical)

Maria Callas
(Focused)

Emily Post
(Proper)

William Shakespeare
(Structured)

Michaelangelo
(Detailed)

Marie Curie
(Tenacious)

Johann Sebastian Bach
(Perfectionist)

Confucius
(Logical)

Implementing The Personality Compass:
If You Are an EAST
(Dominant or Subdominant)

What Is Implementation?

Implementation is simply "putting into action", or using something for a particular purpose. *The Personality Compass* is a resource that simplifies the complexities of human behavior so that you can more easily understand yourself and the people around you. *The Personality Compass* also provides practical implementation exercises for you to use on a daily basis to help you develop and improve the entire gamut of personality traits and aptitudes. You can use this handbook for three very specific and useful purposes.

Use *The Personality Compass* to Achieve Results

- Develop a well-rounded balance of qualities and skills in yourself and increase your own self-esteem.

- Become an astute, other-oriented communicator and enrich all of your personal and professional relationships.

- Enhance both the breadth and depth of your competencies and increase your success on the job and in your daily life.

Using the Compass to Improve EASTS

What To Do If You Are an EAST

EASTS must learn to think and act WEST:
- To achieve well-rounded balance
- When communicating with WESTS
- In situations, jobs or tasks that require WEST attributes and skills

Know what's in it for EASTS to think and act WEST:
- You will improve your effectiveness in relaxing around people
- You will become more flexible and adaptable
- You will increase your ability to be well-rounded
- You will learn to value and develop your weaknesses
- You will get out of your comfort zone and grow
- You will develop self-esteem and power by accomplishing more

Think about the core of the WEST nature:
- WESTS have a free-spirited and flexible nature
- WESTS are carefree, unstructured and creative
- WESTS genuinely enjoy juggling many jobs at once
- WESTS love to take risks and try innovative ideas
- WESTS avoid rules, routine and details
- WESTS are fun-loving and adventurous
- WESTS try never to worry about anything

Tips for EASTS on
How to Act More WEST

Step 1 Study the WEST sections and Chapter Six of this book.

Step 2 Think of WESTS you know, and ask yourself what they might say or do.

Step 3 Make a concentrated effort to think and act as if you are a dominant WEST.

Step 4 Force yourself to view the world and the people you meet from a WEST perspective.

Step 5 Practice! Practice! Practice! WEST behavior and skills can be learned.

Step 6 Start simply, using the following specific guidelines.

How to Act WEST Step-by-Step

Directions: place a cross (X) *in the blank(s) you need to strengthen, then practice.*

- [ ] Dress casually or with a creative flair
- [ ] Loosen up and enjoy each moment with a sense of humor
- [ ] Do at least one thing per week that you have never done before
- [ ] Forget the words "No" and "Why?"
- [ ] Develop an "anything goes" attitude (within reason, of course)
- [ ] Be spontaneous and free-spirited
- [ ] Remove all limits from your dreams (go for them all!)
- [ ] Create change just for the heck of it
- [ ] Put some fun in your life every day
- [ ] Get rid of your safety nets and take some risks
- [ ] Walk with a bounce and exude enthusiasm
- [ ] Explore new ideas and methodologies
- [ ] Expand your horizons way beyond your comfort zone
- [ ] Rebel against the status quo
- [ ] Try a jillion things without worrying about failing or finishing

Specify What You Need

Evaluation Chart for EASTS

Using the preceding pages as guidelines, list below the behaviors you need to develop first.

Example: _Spontaneity_

- _____
- _____

- _____
- _____
- _____

List below a strategy to achieve each of the above.

Example: _Trust myself to go with the flow_

- _____
- _____
- _____
- _____

Identify a WEST person you admire and four characteristics they have that you want/need. Name _____

- _____
- _____

- _____
- _____

Become What You Are Not

Chart For EASTS to Track Your Progress

Directions: Track your behavior improvements in the chart below. Use a cross (X) to indicate status.

Behaviors I have strengthened	Improved in one week	Improved in one month
Watched typical WESTS	☐	☐
Exhibited enthusiasm	☐	☐
Bent the rules	☐	☐
Discussed ideas	☐	☐
Developed open-mindedness	☐	☐
Said I'll try it	☐	☐
Expressed humor	☐	☐
Stopped nagging	☐	☐
Accepted new methods	☐	☐
Became more laid-back	☐	☐
Dared to imagine	☐	☐
Enjoyed the moment	☐	☐
Put adventures into my life	☐	☐
Took a risk	☐	☐
Didn't criticize	☐	☐
Showed adaptability	☐	☐

Behaviors I have strengthened	Improved in one week	Improved in one month
Gave up perfectionism	☐	☐
Developed vision	☐	☐
Worked less	☐	☐
Ceased worrying	☐	☐
Laughed a little (or a lot!)	☐	☐
Set aside inhibitions	☐	☐
Improvised	☐	☐

Resources I have implemented	Implemented in one week	Implemented in one month
Mentored with a WEST	☐	☐
Read about WESTS	☐	☐
Observed many WEST	☐	☐
Learned to value WESTS	☐	☐
Practiced being WEST	☐	☐

Using the Personality Compass to Improve EAST Relationships

Understanding the EAST "Blind Spot"

Stand in one place and hold your head perfectly still, facing straight ahead. Roll your eyes as far to the left and right as possible, and note exactly what lies within your realm of vision. That which lies just beyond what you can see in your peripheral vision is known as your "blind spot." It is there, but you simply can't see it.

Human nature also has "blind spots." You can see things in others that they do not see in themselves – and others can see things in you that you have trouble seeing in yourself.

The most common "blind spot" in EASTS, which can cause problems for themselves and others, is putting high expectations as a top priority. They don't perceive themselves as perfection-obsessed, yet it is at the core of their nature.

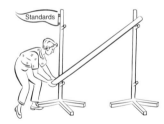

EAST Standards Can Hurt Relationships

Sharon was appalled when her teenage son and his teacher met with her and requested that she ease up on placing so much pressure on Rick to make A grades. Didn't teachers these days realize that colleges have become highly competitive, and if Rick doesn't graduate near the top of his class, he may not be accepted at a top university? How can a teacher in high school be so stupid? And what could she possibly understand about Rick's needs and fears? She's known him for only a few months. Rick couldn't possibly be afraid of his own mother. His problem with nerves is no doubt the result of that neurotic girlfriend of his, not his mother's efforts to help him become a success in life.

Perception: The Root of Most Problems

Rick's perception
- Rick wants to please his mother and do well in school, but no matter how hard he tries, making straight A grades is just too hard for him, so he feels like a failure.
- Rick understands the need to do well in high school in order to get into college, but he doesn't care about attending a top Ivy League school – that's his mother's expectation.
- Rick loves his mother and wants to please her, but that effort is creating health problems (the school nurse suspects stomach ulcers). He feels pressured.

Sharon's perception
- Sharon loves Rick and wants him to have all the opportunities she missed in life by marrying young and not finishing her education.
- Sharon knows that school is difficult for Rick, but she feels that he will thank her someday for forcing him to work hard and fulfill his potential for a good future.
- Sharon is convinced that the best schools provide the best opportunities for the best jobs. So, if it takes A grades to get Rick a scholarship, so be it.

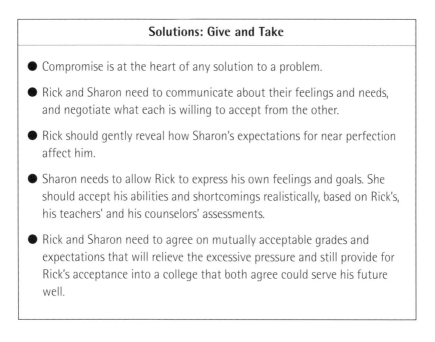

Solutions: Give and Take

● Compromise is at the heart of any solution to a problem.

● Rick and Sharon need to communicate about their feelings and needs, and negotiate what each is willing to accept from the other.

● Rick should gently reveal how Sharon's expectations for near perfection affect him.

● Sharon needs to allow Rick to express his own feelings and goals. She should accept his abilities and shortcomings realistically, based on Rick's, his teachers' and his counselors' assessments.

● Rick and Sharon need to agree on mutually acceptable grades and expectations that will relieve the excessive pressure and still provide for Rick's acceptance into a college that both agree could serve his future well.

Questions & Answers About the EAST Personality

Question   Why do some EASTS get so upset over such trivial matters as leaving a few dirty dishes on the countertop, or leaving shoes by the front door, or a couple of misspelled words in a paper or letter?

Answer   *To an EAST nature that is innately logical and tidy, these are not trivial matters. In the EAST type brain, it simply makes sense to clean up after yourself, to put things where they belong, and to look up the correct spelling of a word. In EAST reasoning, it takes less energy to do something right the first time than it does to do it halfway, or wrong, and then have to finish it later or do it over again. EASTS are not comfortable in a messy environment, and errors seem to stand out like neon lights in their heads. Keep in mind that EASTS can't really help their nature – but they can and should learn to "go WEST" when these characteristics become more unproductive and tedious than beneficial for themselves and others.*

Question   Why do some EASTS have a way of making others feel inferior, as if they never quite measure up – and not only do they sometimes criticize what people do, but even the way they go about doing it?

Answer   *Most EASTS don't mean to make people feel inadequate, nor do they intentionally criticize. Because their analytical nature focuses on the most efficient way to achieve quality, and their brain breaks processes into sequential steps needed to achieve best results, most EASTS*

actually believe they are being helpful when they offer their unsolicited advice on how to do something better. However, that information is not always appreciated by a non-EAST who doesn't perceive their message in that light.

Question   **Why do some EASTS get into an argument and hang on to it like a pit bull terrier, refusing to drop the subject long after it has run its course?**

Answer   *The EAST analytical brain works much like a computer, with one logical point after another popping up methodically, sequentially, and usually in great detail, to prove their line of reasoning. EASTS don't necessarily intend to be antagonistic, but some EASTS have trouble knowing when their point has been sufficiently made. At the extreme level, they get so caught up in the details of the reasoning process that they can't stop midstream, even if the situation warrants it. Sometimes it's as if their brain is on automatic pilot and the program must run its course, regardless of the circumstances. More well-rounded EASTS learn how to build their argumentation to an impressive crescendo and then stop while they are ahead.*

Chapter Five

Valuing the Nature of SOUTH

The Uniqueness of SOUTH

Typical SOUTH
- Team player, gregarious
- Friendly, likable
- Slow, laid-back
- Good listener, sympathetic
- Peace-loving, kind
- Helpful, hospitable
- Caring, nurturing
- Understanding, patient
- Generous, giving
- Process-centered

Extreme SOUTH
- Dependent, shy
- Procrastinator, lackadaisical
- Non-assertive, meek
- Complainer, whiner
- Insecure, frightened
- Easily hurt, withdrawn
- Martyr, vulnerable
- Overzealous to please
- Easily intimidated
- Clinging, possessive

SOUTHS at a Glance

"SOUTHS Do It with Feeling"

- **Motto** SOUTHS build the best teams
- **Symbol** Sunshine
- **Greatest strength** Cooperation
- **Basic weakness** Non-assertiveness
- **Fundamental aptitude** Peace-making
- **Priority** Values
- **Motivational turn-on** Helping
- **Pet peeve** Conflict
- **Work and play style** Group
- **Main work competency** Teambuilding
- **Pace** Slow and laid-back
- **Image** Compassion

SOUTH Role Model

It is inspirational that as Pope John Paul II visits various countries around the world, he is often described as a pilgrim of peace, for he encourages understanding among people everywhere. This pilgrim Pope urges every individual to have the strong values of goodness, justice, civic virtue and freedom as he works hard to spread world peace.

Top 10 Super Strengths of SOUTHS

Typical SOUTHS might often exhibit:

1 Cooperation
2 Peacefulness
3 Fairness
4 Helpfulness
5 Volunteerism
6 Diplomacy
7 Patience
8 Loyalty
9 Unselfishness
10 Sensitivity

SOUTHS Can Take Time

Michael is a SOUTH Director of Health and Human Development for a large tool and die company. His thirty years with the same company reflect his corporate loyalty, as well as his need for security. A beloved employee, Michael is known by almost all of the three hundred co-workers at his plant site. The main reason, of course, is that Michael takes the time to listen, to inquire about the people and their families, to help in any way it might be needed, to show sincere concern for others, to spend time enjoying people and reflecting their value by the time he spends with them. "I love everybody," he says.

From Super Strengths to Team Stars

How SOUTHS Charge-Up a Team

Most SOUTHS naturally help the teams they are on by:

- Building team cohesiveness
- Motivating team players to work together
- Raising individual and team loyalty levels
- Increasing team cooperation
- Developing team spirit
- Turning individual insecurity into team support
- Instilling a team positive attitude
- Inspiring their team to believe in the possibility of success
- Prioritizing the value of people above all else
- Helping/coaching their team to victory

When SOUTH Team Leadership Works Best
The SOUTH democratic leadership style is most effective when:

- independent or experienced individuals or teams need to make their own decisions about what to do and how to do it;
- mature, well-behaved individuals or teams need someone to listen to all perspectives.

Top 10 Danger Zones of SOUTHS

Extreme SOUTHS might often exhibit:

1 Indecision
2 Dependence
3 Insecurity
4 Slowness
5 Fear
6 Non-assertiveness
7 Over-sensitivity
8 Self-pity
9 Excuses
10 Complaining

SOUTHS Can Take Blame

On a bad day, Mary is a non-assertive sales clerk who gets blamed by her boss for spending too much time talking with each customer and not hustling more sales, for not quickly re-straightening the shelves between customers, for taking too long on her breaks and for constantly asking a co-worker to help her ring up her sales on the new computer. Her friend in another department noticed, "Mary sells more than anyone in her department because people like her. She's always pleasant and helpful. I wish she would stand up for herself, though, and stop accepting the blame for everything that isn't perfect over there."

From Danger Zones to Dynamite

- SOUTH *indecision* and *dependence* can sometimes result in prevention of errors and prevention of breaches in protocol.

  When it is not perfectly clear which decision or action is best, SOUTHS can often gain approval by checking with those in charge before mistakes are made.

- SOUTH *insecurity* and *slowness* can sometimes result in high quality.

  SOUTHS like to please and can be so eager to get approval that they will take special care and time to do particularly good work.

- SOUTH *fear* and *non-assertiveness* can sometimes result in extra precautions that improve safety.

  When potentially dangerous or intimidating situations occur, SOUTHS can often prevent disaster by holding back and not doing or saying anything.

- SOUTH *over-sensitivity* and *self-pity* can sometimes result in helping those around them to become more other-oriented, which improves communication and relationships.

  When tasks begin to take on greater importance than the people who perform them, SOUTHS have a way of forcing others to consider the impact of their behavior on people's feelings because it is difficult for them to hide their hurt.

- SOUTH *excuses* and *complaining* can sometimes result in greater awareness of possible road-blocks to goal achievement.

  When SOUTHS complain about problems, it forces others to focus on ways to remove the obstacles that create them and make poor results possible.

Understanding the Differences Between SOUTH-EASTS and SOUTH-WESTS

The relationship between the four cultural natures and the North, East, South and West cultures that *The Personality Compass* shows us makes it easy to identify and remember the natural qualities and abilities that people within the four main compass directions possess. SOUTH people have characteristics similar to those in South cultures and, if we can also identify their subdominant natures, which will always be adjacent on the Compass, we can learn much more about them.

Ray and Lisa: Alike and Different

Most of Lisa's qualities she has in common with South cultures, and her next highest number in common with East cultures. She is a dominant SOUTH-subdominant EAST. Lisa and Ray, a dominant SOUTH–subdominant WEST, have much in common as they share SOUTH qualities. They are also different in many ways, because of their opposite subdominant natures.

Both the dominant and subdominant natures can have a significant impact on the types of tasks that appeal to an individual, as well as on the aptitudes required to achieve quality and excellence at the tasks. Lisa, a SOUTH-EAST, is friendly, caring, structured, detailed and organized. Ray, a SOUTH-WEST, is friendly, caring, flexible, creative and adventurous. Their interests and talents differ somewhat and they are not equally suited to the same job, even though both are dominant SOUTHS.

SOUTH-EAST People

Friendly • Caring • Structured • Detailed • Organized

SOUTH-WEST People

Friendly • Caring • Flexible • Creative • Adventurous

Recognizing SOUTH Behaviors

Twenty or more crosses (X) indicate a strong SOUTH nature.

SOUTHS in general . . .

- [ ] Talk, move and eat slowly
- [ ] Avoid holding direct eye contact
- [ ] Shake hands softly
- [ ] Speak in a friendly manner
- [ ] Sound quieter than most
- [ ] Lean their head and shoulders in toward others
- [ ] Avoid drawing attention to themselves
- [ ] Wear light, pastel colors or rich earth tones
- [ ] Listen with genuine interest
- [ ] Appear unassuming and congenial
- [ ] Exhibit an unselfish caring about people
- [ ] Are sensitive to others feelings
- [ ] Prefer following to leading
- [ ] Show up late at times

- [ ] Like to communicate when not too shy
- [ ] Dislike friction or conflict
- [ ] Work more from necessity than pleasure
- [ ] Praise others first
- [ ] Put values as a top priority
- [ ] Find criticism personally painful
- [ ] Make excellent team players
- [ ] Have limitless patience
- [ ] Seek others' advice before acting
- [ ] Need approval and support
- [ ] Hate having to make decisions
- [ ] Can take on a martyr role at times
- [ ] Encourage others to feel good about themselves
- [ ] Believe in democratic problem-solving
- [ ] Volunteer for everything
- [ ] Give gifts with no expectations
- [ ] Respect authority and try to please
- [ ] Exude kindness, generosity, humility
- [ ] Offer excuses when things go wrong
- [ ] Value peace, loyalty and cooperation

Recognizing SOUTH Children

Typical SOUTH Children in General...
- Cooperate in helping others of all ages
- Eat, drink and move slowly
- Go to bed without a fight
- Get pleasure from sharing their toys
- Play well with other children
- Make friends easily
- Take their time in trying to walk
- Show affection with hugs and kisses
- Play by others' rules
- Like school and its social activities

Carrie liked to be held and cuddled from the day she was born. She rarely cried unless she was hungry, and exhibited none of the temper tantrums some of her playmates used to have in order to get their own way. Her parents called her their "golden child" because she seemed to sparkle. Always smiling and cheerful, she loved to help with everything, and she would rather her friends have the toy they wanted than have it herself.

Extreme SOUTH Children in General…

- Cry when they are hurt or tired
- Let other children boss them around
- Whine and beg for what they want
- Seem to have nightmares
- Can be painfully shy and introverted
- Cling to people who make them feel safe
- Appear afraid of strangers or new activities
- Dislike school because they fear failure
- Will settle for what others don't want

Tommy often embarrassed his macho father because he screamed every time he took the slightest fall. He was afraid to jump into his father's arms at the pool, and he refused to try any kind of sport. The saddest part of the story is that the more upset the father became by his son's behavior, the more insecure and withdrawn Tommy became.

Recognizing SOUTHS in Different Roles

As Students
SOUTHS in General...

- Hesitate to speak out in class
- Trust others' opinions more than their own
- Avoid taking sides in controversial issues
- Aim to be liked, and are often popular
- Respect the instructor's authority
- Try not to be too noticeable
- Enjoy a slow-speed, relaxed environment
- Display very little competitive spirit
- Turn assignments in late at times
- Dread class presentations
- Say as little as possible in discussions
- Have many friends

As Athletes
SOUTHS in General...

- Make loyal team players
- Do what they can to help the team
- Try to keep harmony among players
- Enjoy the team spirit, win or lose
- Feel terrible if they hurt the team
- Have trouble maintaining vigorous workouts
- Accept victories with humility
- Become discouraged easily, so appreciate team support
- Need a great deal of confidence-building
- Get more nervous than most in competitions
- Do whatever the coach says
- Exhibit pride in teammates more than in themselves

As Leaders
SOUTHS in General...

- Employ a democratic leadership style
- Share authority willingly
- Seek input as to what should be done
- Depend on others to do much of the work
- Get upset in a crisis or conflict
- Create a laid-back, friendly atmosphere
- Keep channels of communication open
- Allow for group decision-making
- Listen to all perspectives of an issue
- Give requests more than orders
- Try to please and be liked by everyone
- Reward cooperation and commitment

As Friends, Spouses or Parents
SOUTHS in General...

- Like to give gifts and attention to others
- Are accommodating of others' needs
- Provide a sympathetic ear for troubles
- Are helpful and generous
- Ask and expect little from others
- Feel closest to those who need them
- Will often give in to what others want
- Put spending time with loved ones as a priority
- Avoid conflict whenever possible
- Express feelings more easily than opinions
- Exhibit loyalty and devotion
- Tell others what they want to hear

Recognizing SOUTHS in Different Situations

At Home
SOUTHS in General . . .

- Are nurturing care-takers
- Enjoy giving and receiving open displays of affection
- Need to feel a partner can help take care of them
- Love to be needed by their family
- Work, play and love with emotion
- Will let tasks go to spend time with family
- Display family photos and mementos prominently
- Sacrifice unselfishly for loved ones
- Wait on others without complaint
- Dislike having to take disciplinary action
- Seek help in emergencies
- Shower the family with special treats/efforts

In a Social Environment
SOUTHS in General . . .

- Enjoy being in familiar groups of people
- Attract people like magnets because they're friendly
- Try not to be conspicuous
- Make others feel important
- Focus conversations on family/personal topics
- Prefer staying in a comfortable corner
- Wish they could feel totally confident
- Gravitate toward people who are smiling
- May be uncomfortable eating in public
- Are sensitive to what others say /do
- Use the opportunity to build relationships
- Help clean up and send a thank-you

During an Interview
SOUTHS in General . . .

- Could be a few minutes late, but will offer a reason
- Make intermittent eye contact
- May be first to extend hand for handshake
- Wait for instruction to be seated
- Speak mostly when spoken to, unless encouraged
- Are humble about their accomplishments
- Show interest in opportunities for teamwork
- Speak softly and are careful not to interrupt
- Ask about the people they might be working with
- Like to talk about their family
- Appear a bit nervous
- Let the interviewer have control

On the Job
SOUTHS in General . . .

- Work best when they are not rushed
- Are more people-centered than task-centered
- Need plenty of lead time to meet deadlines
- Offer to help others without being asked
- Enjoy building relationships with co-workers
- Have trouble saying "no", even when overloaded
- Exhibit patience and tolerance
- Prefer to work on teams
- Avoid conflict at almost any cost
- Become embarrassed by praise or compliments (but need both)
- May hold back and let others get recognition
- Wait to be told what to do

Common Comments That Recognize Typical SOUTHS

"*Chris is the best friend I ever had. I know that he will be there for me, no matter what happens. If I call him at 3:00 am and tell him I need to talk, he comes right over – and he usually picks up some doughnuts and hot chocolate on the way. No matter what I say or do, I know he will care about me anyway. He supports my feelings and decisions, even if he doesn't always agree with them.*"

Debra E.

"*Patty is a saint! She has had terrible luck, yet she stays so positive. When other people should be helping her out, she is the one volunteering at the hospital, collecting clothes and food for the underprivileged, and assisting with Meals on Wheels. Her smile and attitude toward life are an inspiration to everyone she meets.*"

Barbara Z.

"*Katie is one of those moms that makes me feel like a failure. She always has fresh-baked cookies for the kids, makes most of her children's clothes and costumes, teaches a Sunday School class, drives the car for the entire neighborhood, and never has a mean word to say about anyone.*"

Lydia A.

Common Comments That Recognize Extreme SOUTHS

"*Dennis upsets us because he lets his wife walk all over him. The more demanding and humiliating she becomes, the more he does for her – cooking, babysitting, laundry, housework, repairs, errands – and he still holds down a full-time job while she shops and plays bridge.*"

Pete and Janice F.

"*Connie has been a friend of mine for a long time, but I must admit that her habit of whining and complaining is really getting to me. She's become a hypochondriac and can't wait to tell me about every new ache and pain she has each day. Of course, she's totally overloaded at work and is sure her boss is deliberately picking on her. Her 'poor me' attitude is annoying because she actually is healthy and has a great job.*"

Eleanor G

"*I wish Joann could see how beautiful and talented she is. Her insecurities and shyness prevent her from even trying to have a serious relationship or a fulfilling job. Everyone sees her potential, except Joann.*"

Nicole P

Motivating SOUTHS for Success

Tell SOUTHS that there is conflict somewhere, and they won't rest until it is resolved. Tell them that you appreciate their help and loyalty, and they will unobtrusively spread their contagious positive attitude, even to the most stubborn hardliners. Tell them you need their teambuilding expertise, and SOUTHS will turn a diverse, sometimes hostile group of individuals into a cohesive unit of cooperative and loyal team players. Tell SOUTHS that they will have a friendly, low-stress and slow-paced work environment, and there is no doubt that they will be happy, committed workers who will do their best to please their bosses and co-workers, and lend an extra helping hand along the way.

What "Turns On" SOUTHS

- Cooperation
- Pleasant people
- Volunteerism
- Optimism
- Slow pace
- Feeling needed
- Communication
- Personal approval
- Teamwork
- Helping others
- Loyalty/trust
- Few pressures
- Kindness
- Smooth sailing
- Following a leader
- Encouragement
- Peacefulness
- Camaraderie
- Emotional support
- Relationships
- Teaching/advising
- Resolving conflicts
- Friendliness
- Low stress

Disclosing SOUTH Pet Peeves

SOUTHS are turned off by anything which they perceive as rude or insensitive. They have little tolerance for aggressive, self-centered behavior, particularly when it can hurt or embarrass others. It is best not to rush SOUTHS. They function best in an easy-going, low-key environment where they can take their time. Put people first when dealing with SOUTHS, and communicate with them in a warm and friendly manner. Never ignore SOUTHS, or fail to speak to them, no matter how preoccupied you might be, because they will feel hurt and spend hours or weeks wondering what they did to make you angry with them. SOUTHS can make invaluable contributions so long as they are not made to feel insecure.

What "Turns Off" SOUTHS

- Shouting
- Feeling shunned
- Conflict
- Negative attitude
- Isolation
- Heavy responsibilities
- Making decisions
- Insensitivity
- Pressure
- Controversy
- Roadblocks to peace
- Lack of teamwork
- Hurried pace
- Competition
- Impatience
- Deadlines
- Being spotlighted
- Uncooperativeness
- Rudeness
- Work overload

Igniting SOUTHS

SOUTHS Are Excited By . . .

- Shared ethical values
- Selling something they believe in
- Democratic processes
- Feeling part of a unified team
- Working together cooperatively
- Opportunities to be of genuine help
- Being around positive people
- People who need and appreciate them
- Doing nice things for others
- Helping resolve conflict

SOUTHS Love To . . .

- Volunteer their service
- Solve people problems
- Build relationships
- Talk with friends
- Please others
- Make other people look good
- Give credit to those who deserve it
- Shower people with praise and gifts
- Take their time
- Feel comfortable and secure

Rewarding SOUTHS

Listed below are a variety of things that SOUTHS find rewarding. They can be used at home or at work as reinforcers to strengthen SOUTH performances.

- Thank yous and appreciation
- A personal invitation to join in
- Handmade gifts
- Sentimental mementos
- Flowers or candy
- Reduced work load
- Help to perform tasks
- More time off
- Social gathering of their friends
- A place on the team
- Membership in a special organization
- Being told how helpful they have been
- One-on-one praise
- Contributions to their favorite charities
- Listening to them with understanding
- Friendly and patient attitudes
- Taking their questions seriously
- Personal gifts that show thought
- Significant photographs
- Written letters of gratitude

Cushioning Clashes with SOUTHS

Clashes occur when different people, ideas or things make contact and create friction or conflict. The greater the difference, the greater is the conflict. Many clashes among people are caused by differences in priorities. Remember:

- GOALS are naturally important to NORTHS
- FACTS are naturally important to EASTS
- VALUES are naturally important to SOUTHS
- METHODS are naturally important to WESTS

People clash most often over that which is naturally most important to them. Two or more SOUTHS might clash over differing values. SOUTHS and EASTS might clash when values conflict with facts. SOUTHS and WESTS might clash when values conflict with methods, and SOUTHS and NORTHS might clash when values conflict with goals.

Natural Clashes Between Opposites

SOUTHS	vs	NORTHS
People-centered	vs	Task-centered
Laid-back	vs	Hardworking
Team players	vs	Independent
Emotional	vs	Practical
Democratic leaders	vs	Authoritarian leaders
Personable	vs	Business-like
Helpful	vs	Controlling
Slow-paced	vs	Fast-paced

How to Avoid Conflict with SOUTHS

- Share their values
- Don't rush them
- Stay relaxed
- Let them help
- Value people
- Minimize pressure
- Inspire trust
- Look for the positive
- Show understanding
- Include them
- Don't embarrass them

- Think of others
- Smile a lot
- Meet their needs
- Don't yell
- Be diplomatic
- Overlook tardiness
- Act friendly
- Be a team player
- Socialize
- Nurture

- Be cooperative
- Learn to listen
- Help them
- Show sensitivity
- Avoid conflict
- Sacrifice ego
- Work together
- Keep stress low
- Communicate often
- Empathize
- Exhibit compassion

Do's and Don'ts of Living or Working with SOUTHS

Do's

- Do – be sensitive to SOUTHS' feelings
- Do – appreciate the SOUTH need to be helpful
- Do – help SOUTHS feel valued
- Do –thank SOUTHS for all they do
- Do – recognize SOUTHS' need for peace and approval
- Do – encourage SOUTHS to finish what they start
- Do – give SOUTHS lead time to complete tasks
- Do – take time to chat with SOUTHS
- Do – show friendliness and patience with SOUTHS
- Do – treat SOUTHS gently for best performance

Give SOUTHS What they Need

As a SOUTH Administrative Assistant, Troy tried his best to make life for his boss as smooth and easy as possible. He enjoyed thinking of ways to please Mr Tucker, and, in fact, went far beyond the call of duty by running personal errands, stocking favorite snacks, and obtaining tickets for special sports events for his boss. Troy thrived on the gratitude often expressed for his efforts. The more approval he received from Mr Tucker, the more Troy did to be helpful.

Don'ts

- Don't – let SOUTHS depend on you too much
- Don't – expect consistent promptness from SOUTHS
- Don't – be embarrassed by SOUTHS' help and gift-giving
- Don't – allow SOUTHS to wallow in self-pity
- Don't – openly reprimand SOUTHS
- Don't – complain about people around SOUTHS
- Don't – show disregard for feelings
- Don't – fight with SOUTHS – talk it out calmly
- Don't – rush SOUTHS to a high-stress level
- Don't – ask SOUTHS for high-pressure speed

Don't Take SOUTHS for Granted

Although Gayle enjoyed doing special favors and preparing special surprises for her family, she was beginning to feel like a hired hand. There was a time that she prepared the family's favorite treats and they responded with special hugs and thank-yous. Now they seemed irritated if special goodies were not in their lunches at least twice a week. Gayle was beginning to realize that giving to people who appreciated it felt a lot better than giving to those who expected or demanded her favors.

"Best Bets" for Compatibility with SOUTHS

Take note spouses, children, friends, bosses and co-workers of SOUTHS! A quick compatibility check will help you identify those who tend to get along best with SOUTH people.

Personality types that are adjacent to SOUTH on the Personality Compass (EAST and WEST) are naturally most compatible with SOUTHS. The highest degree of compatibility usually occurs when both the dominant and subdominant natures are adjacent on the Compass, as illustrated below.

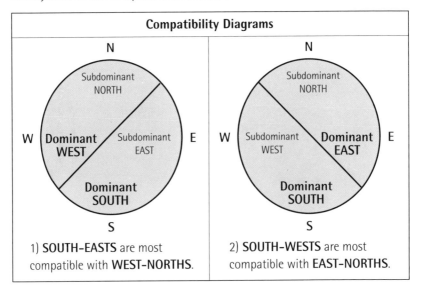

Compatibility Diagrams

1) **SOUTH-EASTS** are most compatible with **WEST-NORTHS**.

2) **SOUTH-WESTS** are most compatible with **EAST-NORTHS**.

"Cash In" on Compatibility with SOUTHS

1) SOUTH-EASTS and WEST-NORTHS complement each other by completing the circle of qualities and talents that create well-rounded individuals and teams.

2) SOUTH-WESTS and EAST-NORTHS also function together productively because their natures are different, but not opposite, so they enrich each other.

SOUTHS are not generally compatible with dominant NORTHS because they are opposite in nature and have very little in common, unless both types are well-rounded individuals.

SOUTHS are usually compatible with other dominant SOUTHS because they have similar interests and abilities, but they need other types to help them achieve their fullest potential.

Tips for SOUTHS to Get Along with Others

Directions: SOUTHS, cross (X) off as you conquer each skill

- [ ] Finish faster
- [ ] Don't be overly sensitive
- [ ] Be quicker to take action
- [ ] Develop a tougher mental attitude
- [ ] Speed up everything you do
- [ ] Ask for help when you need it
- [ ] Help yourself as much as you help others
- [ ] Don't feel you must give gifts to be liked
- [ ] Do more on your own, independently
- [ ] Trust your own abilities
- [ ] Show up on time and be prepared
- [ ] Talk less when you should be working
- [ ] Express honest opinions when appropriate
- [ ] Get to the point quickly
- [ ] Offer fewer explanations or excuses
- [ ] Don't be afraid of disagreements
- [ ] Be more assertive
- [ ] Make quicker, firmer decisions

- [ ] Exhibit confidence
- [ ] Meet deadlines
- [ ] Don't let burdens drag you down
- [ ] Watch becoming overly friendly or ingratiating
- [ ] Accept credit, compliments, praise and gifts graciously
- [ ] React less emotionally to difficulties
- [ ] Keep perceived slights in perspective
- [ ] Don't try quite so hard to please

- [ ] Complete tasks that need to be done
- [ ] Develop a professional demeanor
- [ ] Avoid the tendency to "smother"
- [ ] Make only promises you can keep
- [ ] Don't be a martyr
- [ ] Procrastinate and complain less
- [ ] Take the initiative

SOUTHS, Beware!

When a person or situation causes you to feel hurt or worried, and you find yourself wanting to withdraw into yourself and become a silent martyr, break into tears, or begin to whine or complain, STOP! Many SOUTHS seem to feel that the more vulnerable they appear, the more support they will receive from others. That tactic might work briefly with other SOUTHS, but even they tire of it eventually.

Targeting SOUTHS for the Right Job

Terrific Jobs for SOUTHS

- Administrative Assistant
- Salesperson
- Human Resources Rep
- Family Doctor/Nurse
- Diplomat
- Psychologist
- Counselor
- Teacher
- Mediator

- Receptionist
- Telephone Operator
- Public Relations Rep
- Assistant Coach
- Missionary
- Waiter
- Social Worker
- Minister
- Bartender

Memory Jogger

You need SOUTHS on the job when . . .

- You need teamwork and cooperation
- You need someone to diffuse conflict
- You need a person to make a friendly impression
- You need a slow-paced, relaxed atmosphere
- You need a loyal follower

Fine-Tuning for SOUTH Jobs

Regina is a dominant SOUTH-subdominant EAST nature. She is the perfect family doctor because she loves helping people and working closely with families as a cohesive unit. She provides her patients with a custom-designed nutrition chart, individualized exercise program and scheduled yearly examinations.

William is a dominant SOUTH-subdominant WEST nature. He is the perfect diplomat because he is friendly and gregarious, is a good listener who enjoys focusing on others, he cares about helping people as a representative of his country's "team", is flexible, can adapt to other customs easily, and he is a creative problem-solver.

5 Jobs for SOUTH–EAST People
1 Human Resources Rep – people person (S), organized (E)
2 Family Doctor/Nurse – caring (S), detailed (E)
3 Mediator – peace-loving (S), structured (E)
4 Receptionist – friendly (S), logical (E)
5 Assistant Coach – team player (S), strategist (E)

Jobs for SOUTH–WEST People
1 Salesperson – likable (S), flexible (W)
2 Diplomat – hospitable (S), adaptable (W)
3 Missionary – giving (S), adventurous (W)
4 Waiter – helpful (S), fast-paced (W)
5 Bartender – good listener (S), sense of humor (W)

Why SOUTHS Make Great Employees

When a job requires SOUTH communication and people skills, no one can do it like a SOUTH. If SOUTHS are not given the opportunity to relate frequently with people, they will do it anyway, because they can't help it. They need people as profoundly as they need air. Failing to use their sincere desire to help others, and their special gifts for resolving conflicts and creating goodwill among all types of people would be a mistake, because SOUTHS can be responsible for inspiring a pleasant work environment of loyal, cohesive team players.

SOUTHS Can Win People Over

Hal knew the moment he met Jack that he would be perfect as the Public Relations Liaison. His smile was electric and he was like a magnet. People were immediately drawn to his warmth and friendliness. Hal watched as people surrounded Jack, and he marveled at the way Jack listened intently to each person as if the two of them were alone in the room. It was remarkable. Jack seemed sincerely interested when he asked Hal about his family, hobbies, his favorite sports teams, and his best golf game. Hal felt as if he had known Jack all of his life.

SOUTHS Love to Help

Marilyn was thrilled when she learned of her promotion to Staff Development Trainer. She had given a great deal of thought to programs that could benefit the employees – programs like departmental teambuilding, health and fitness, child care, on-site evening classes and many others. She wanted to establish as many opportunities as possible to help the employees get together and feel part of the team.

SOUTHS Hate to Work Alone

Daniel, a SOUTH sociologist, decorated his small office with framed "words of wisdom" that reflected his belief that teamwork and friendship were the strongest warriors against human loneliness, depression and stagnation. A few large examples, in particular, stood out among dozens.

- Teamwork works
- Share the load – it's lighter
- He's not heavy, he's my brother
- It takes a friend to be a friend
- Reach out and touch someone

SOUTHS Can Take the Time

Gene noticed that whenever employees had a problem, they were being sent to him. Since he worked in sales, not in personnel and human resources, Gene questioned his boss as to why this procedure was being followed. The answer shouldn't have been surprising: "Gene," he was told, "you are so good with people. You just have a way with them. You take the time to listen, as well as to help them find solutions, and they always come back happier and more motivated to do their job. I've watched you – you look at the person, not at your watch."

Top 3 Interview Questions & Answers That Help Hire SOUTHS for SOUTH Jobs

1 "Tell me about yourself."

SOUTHS generally like to talk about topics other than themselves, so they might mention such things as:
- How interested they are in this job
- What a terrific facility and company yours appears to be
- The friendliness of the people they've met that day
- Team projects they have worked on
- Interesting clients and co-workers they have worked with
- Volunteer work they have done
- Ways they have helped their boss achieve his or her goals
- Showing an interest in you, your family and your job

2 "What interested you in our company (or the job in question)?"

SOUTH interest is often whetted by:
- Working with reputedly nice people
- A friendly and relaxed work environment
- Low-stress pace and work they feel they can do
- Emphasis on teamwork and cooperation
- Opportunities for security and good family benefits
- Being able to help meet a need
- Democratic processes that ensure fairness
- Sensitivity to the needs and welfare of all employees

3 "Why *should* we hire you?"

SOUTHS will often describe their own professional strengths as:

- Being cooperative
- Being a good listener
- Maintaining a cheerful, positive attitude
- Getting along well with others
- Communicating effectively with diverse types of people
- Going the second mile to help out
- Helping to resolve conflicts and problems
- Having patience with "difficult" people

Famous SOUTHS
(Based on historical perception)

Mother Teresa
(Nurturing)

Albert Schweitzer
(Compassionate)

Mahatma Gandhi
(Non-violent)

Joan of Arc
(Self-sacrificing)

Piotr Tchaikovsky
(Romantic)

Martin Luther King, Jr
(Peaceful)

Elizabeth Barrett Browning
(Sentimental)

Florence Nightingale
(Caring)

Implementing The Personality Compass:
If You Are a SOUTH
(Dominant or Subdominant)

What Is Implementation?

Implementation is simply "putting into action", or using something for a particular purpose. *The Personality Compass* is a resource that simplifies the complexities of human behavior so that you can more easily understand yourself and the people around you. *The Personality Compass* also provides practical implementation exercises for you to use on a daily basis to help you develop and improve the entire gamut of personality traits and aptitudes. You can use this handbook for three very specific and useful purposes.

Use *The Personality Compass* to Achieve Results

- Develop a well-rounded balance of qualities and skills in yourself and increase your own self-esteem.

- Become an astute, other-oriented communicator and enrich all of your personal and professional relationships.

- Enhance both the breadth and depth of your competencies and increase your success on the job and in your daily life.

Using the Compass to Improve SOUTHS

What To Do If You Are a SOUTH

SOUTHS must learn to think and act NORTH:
- To achieve well-rounded balance
- When communicating with NORTHS
- In situations, jobs or tasks that require NORTH attributes and skills

Know what's in it for SOUTHS to think and act NORTH:
- You will improve your effectiveness in managing people
- You will become more assertive and confident
- You will increase your ability to be well-rounded
- You will learn to value and develop your weaknesses
- You will get out of your comfort zone and grow
- You will develop self-esteem and power by accomplishing more

Think about the core of the NORTH nature:
- NORTHS have a strong and independent nature
- NORTHS are fast-paced, assertive and rarely relax
- NORTHS genuinely enjoy working hard and competing
- NORTHS love to be leaders, in charge and have authority
- NORTHS avoid red tape and roadblocks
- NORTHS are decisive and can take initiative
- NORTHS try never to fail or show weakness

Tips for SOUTHS on
How to Act More NORTH

Step 1 Study the NORTH sections and Chapter Three of this book.

Step 2 Think of NORTHS you know, and ask yourself what they might say or do.

Step 3 Make a concentrated effort to think and act as if you are a dominant NORTH.

Step 4 Force yourself to view the world and the people you meet from a NORTH perspective.

Step 5 Practice! Practice! Practice! NORTH behavior and skills can be learned.

Step 6 Start simply, using the following specific guidelines.

How to Act NORTH Step-by-Step

Directions: place a cross (X) *in the blank(s) you need to strengthen, then practice.*

- [ ] Look people directly in the eye
- [ ] Shake hands firmly
- [ ] Talk, move and work fast
- [ ] Set goals – and do what it takes to achieve them
- [ ] Be bold and assertive
- [ ] Stand tall, with confidence
- [ ] Make decisions quickly (trust your instinct!)
- [ ] Enjoy challenges as opportunities
- [ ] Compete to win and be the best
- [ ] Take initiative (just jump in!)
- [ ] Take more control of situations and events
- [ ] Accept leadership roles
- [ ] Speak up and speak out
- [ ] Find ways to get what you want
- [ ] Have the courage to fight for your beliefs

Specify What You Need

Evaluation Chart for SOUTHS

Using the preceding pages as guidelines, list below the behaviors you need to develop first.

Example: _Self-assertion_

- _____   • _____
- _____   • _____
                            • _____

List below a strategy to achieve each of the above.

Example: _When I have an opinion, make sure it gets a proper_
- _hearing._____
- _____
- _____
- _____

Identify a NORTH person you admire and four characteristics they have that you want/need. Name _____

- _____   • _____
- _____   • _____

Become What You Are Not

Chart For SOUTHS to Track Your Progress

Directions: Track your behavior improvements in the chart below. Use a cross (X) to indicate status.

Behaviors I have strengthened	Improved in one week	Improved in one month
Watched typical NORTHS	☐	☐
Became more assertive	☐	☐
Took charge	☐	☐
Speeded up	☐	☐
Worked hard	☐	☐
Exhibited courage	☐	☐
Expressed opinions	☐	☐
Developed leadership	☐	☐
Didn't complain	☐	☐
Made decisions	☐	☐
Showed confidence	☐	☐
Met deadlines	☐	☐
Accepted credit	☐	☐
Stayed on task	☐	☐
Showed initiative	☐	☐
Didn't procrastinate	☐	☐

Behaviors I have strengthened	Improved in one week	Improved in one month
Became more independent	☐	☐
Asked for help	☐	☐
Toughened up	☐	☐
Enjoyed being alone	☐	☐
Avoided excuses	☐	☐
Chatted less	☐	☐
Spoke out	☐	☐

Resources I have implemented	Implemented in one week	Implemented in one month
Mentored a NORTH	☐	☐
Read about NORTHS	☐	☐
Observed many NORTHS	☐	☐
Learned to value NORTHS	☐	☐
Practiced being NORTH	☐	☐

Using the Personality Compass to Improve SOUTH Relationships

Understanding the SOUTH "Blind Spot"

Stand in one place and hold your head perfectly still, facing straight ahead. Roll your eyes as far to the left and right as possible, and note exactly what lies within your realm of vision. That which lies just beyond what you can see in your peripheral vision is known as your "blind spot". It is there, but you simply can't see it.

Human nature also has "blind spots." You can see things in others that they do not see in themselves – and others can see things in you that you have trouble seeing in yourself. The most common "blind spot" in SOUTHS, which can cause problems for themselves and others, is putting their value of devotion to loved ones as a top priority. They don't perceive themselves as people-needy, yet it is at the core of their nature.

SOUTH Insecurities Can Hurt Relationships

It was totally incomprehensible to Carson that his wife, Carla, could sit there and tell their marriage counselor that one of the biggest problems in their marriage was that he loved her too much. How could that be? Of course he wanted to be with Carla every possible minute – he adored her and enjoyed her company. How could she say she felt smothered and imprisoned? If Carla really loved him as much as she said she did, then why didn't she need him as much as he needed her? And why did she become angry when he asked her opinion on everything, as if that were somehow a sign of weakness on his part?

Perception: The Root of Most Problems

Carla's Perception

- Carla loves Carson and enjoys his company, but she also enjoys spending time alone or with her friends.

- Carla respects the fact that Carson loves her and wants to spend time with her, but every spare waking moment is just taking it too far. She feels as if he's attached to her ankle.

- Carla needs Carson to give her some space and find ways to enjoy himself without her presence at all times.

Carson's Perception

- Carson loves Carla and has no need for anyone else in his life, so it's hard for him to understand why he isn't enough for Carla.

- Carson respects Carla's feelings, but it hurts him that she feels that way. He doesn't mean to be a burden to her. He would never consider her a burden, no matter what.

- Carson needs to accept that Carla loves him and enjoys spending time with him, but not feel hurt when she chooses to spend time without him sometimes.

Solutions: Give and Take

● Compromise is at the heart of any solution to a problem.

● Carla and Carson need to communicate about their feelings and needs, and negotiate what each is willing to accept from the other.

● Carla should gently reveal how Carson's need for her 24-hour-a-day devotion affects both of them in an unhealthy way.

● Carson needs to develop more interests so that he does not depend on his wife to fill his time or make him happy. He needs to focus on spending quality time with her and cut back on the quantity of time he needs from her.

● Carla needs to go out of her way to let Carson know how much she loves him, how important he is in her life, and how often she thinks of him when they are apart. She could also give him ideas of ways he might enjoy spending time without her.

Questions & Answers About the SOUTH Personality

Question Why do some SOUTHS find it so difficult to give their honest opinions to others, sometimes expressing their beliefs one way to one person, and then telling another that they feel exactly the opposite way?

Answer *SOUTHS, in general, are people pleasers and peacemakers. They often tell people whatever they think those people want to hear, either because they don't want to hurt their feelings by disagreeing with them, or because they don't want to create conflict. Non-SOUTHS may perceive this tendency as being untruthful at times, but SOUTHS never see their behavior that way. In their minds, they are helping others to feel comfortable and valuable, and they are also saving themselves from the discomfort of not being accepted or approved of, or having to deal with dissension or unpleasantness, which are among their worst nightmares.*

Question Why do some SOUTHS have trouble asserting their authority when they are in a leadership position, whether in the role of a manager or that of being a parent?

Answer *By nature SOUTHS do not truly enjoy having positions of leadership. They much prefer having someone else in charge. However, it is almost impossible to avoid leadership roles from time to time when trying to move forward in a career, or when accepting the responsibility of*

parenthood. Because SOUTHS want to be everyone's friend, and need to be liked, they tend to let others have their way and defer to others' needs and preferences over their own. But when they are in a leadership role, this deference can cause them problems when people begin to take advantage of their generous and giving nature. Then, SOUTHS need to realize that asserting their legitimate authority will only increase the amount of esteem and respect that their subordinates or their children have for them.

Question **How can some SOUTHS, who are typically other-oriented, be so inconsiderate of others by not carrying their full load of the work, and by slowing up the work process by wasting time chit-chatting with people everywhere they go?**

Answer *Most SOUTHS probably have no idea that they are shirking work or slowing up work processes. Their perception of a lot of work is very different from that of a NORTH or an EAST, and speed is not something that most SOUTHS perceive as a valuable goal. When being true to their natural values, which include showing a personal interest in people, and helping to brighten other people's days, SOUTH friendliness can be viewed as a time-wasting roadblock to speedy goal achievement by non-SOUTHS. It is important to note that SOUTHS who offer a warm smile and a simple hello during work hours, and save conversations for personal time, are far more popular in the workplace than those who are easily side-tracked.*

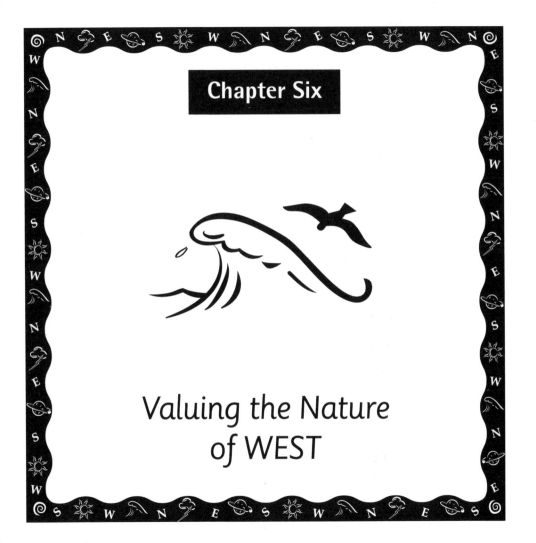

Chapter Six

Valuing the Nature of WEST

The Uniqueness of WEST

Typical WEST
- Risk-taker, adventurous
- Fast, energetic
- Visionary, unconventional
- Innovative, creative
- Flexible, multi-talented
- Juggles many tasks, adaptable
- Spontaneous, unstructured
- Enthusiastic, sense of humor
- Free-spirited, versatile
- Idea-centered, dreamer

Extreme WEST
- Practical joker, silly
- Error-prone, impulsive
- Unfocused, scattered
- Unable to finish, flighty
- Undisciplined, careless
- Often late, irresponsible
- Frivolous, wild and crazy
- Exaggerative, inaccurate
- Superficial, evasive
- Danger-driven

WESTS at a Glance

"WESTS Do It with Imagination"

- **Motto** WESTS expand all horizons
- **Symbol** Wave with soaring bird
- **Greatest strength** Innovative creativity
- **Basic weakness** Disorganization
- **Fundamental aptitude** Seeing the big picture
- **Priority** Methods
- **Motivational turn-on** Freedom
- **Pet peeve** Rules
- **Work and play style** Adaptable
- **Main work competency** Coordinating many tasks
- **Pace** Fast and flexible
- **Image** Originality

WEST Role Model

Stories recount that Pablo Picasso, one of the most renowned artists of modern times, said that while he worked, he left his body outside the door, similar to the way the Moslems remove their shoes before entering the mosque. He tried to cast off all barriers so that pure energy could flow from him to the canvas without limitations or constraints.

Top 10 Super Strengths of WESTS

Typical WESTS might often exhibit:

1 Creativity
2 Innovation
3 Flexibility
4 Vision
5 Broadmindedness
6 Ideas
7 Enthusiasm
8 Motivation
9 Adaptability
10 Curiosity

WESTS Can Take Pressure

Allen is a WEST assistant chef at a major big-city hotel. No matter how busy the restaurant becomes, or how many crises occur, Allen stays calm, cool and collected. He can prepare a dozen different meals simultaneously without panic, moving from one to another at the speed of light, and still create a delectable presentation that adds flair to the flavor. When asked how he takes the frantic pace and pressure, he replies, "What good is worrying? Just enjoy it, whatever happens."

From Super Strengths to Team Stars

How WESTS Charge-Up a Team

Most WESTS naturally help the teams they are on by:

- Building team flexibility
- Motivating team players to make needed changes in strategies
- Raising individual and team enthusiasm levels
- Increasing team creativity
- Developing team vision
- Turning individual conservatism into team desire to take risks
- Keeping each player adaptable enough for reaching the team goal
- Instilling team energy to excel
- Inspiring their team to dream the dream for success
- Daring/cheering their team on to victory

When WEST Team Leadership Works Best

The WEST free-rein leadership style is most effective when:

- independent or experienced individuals or teams need the freedom to do what they want, when they want and how they want;
- free-spirited and creative individuals or teams need to be given the opportunity to follow their vision and instincts, with as few constraints as possible, more or less having a leader "on call".

Top 10 Danger Zones of WESTS

Extreme WESTS might often exhibit:

1 Disorganization
2 Sloppiness
3 Rebelliousness
4 Unpredictability
5 Irresponsibility
6 Recklessness
7 Inattentiveness
8 Boredom
9 Impulsiveness
10 Eccentricity

WESTS Can Take Dangerous Chances

On a bad day, Keith is a reckless entrepreneur who gambles with other people's money in hopes of hitting the big jackpot. He's willing to risk huge debts or bodily harm on the chance that this could be his lucky day. Based on instinct, rather than a logical plan, he flies by the seat of his pants on a day-to-day basis, often looking for the quick buck or the quick fix to a problem.

From Danger Zones to Dynamite

- WEST *disorganization* and *sloppiness* can sometimes result in a comfortable sense of informality.

  When a personal or professional environment becomes tense or rigid, WESTS often have a way of loosening up the atmosphere by not placing importance on appearances or protocol.

- WEST *rebelliousness* and *unpredictability* can sometimes result in improved ways of doing things.

  When the status quo becomes routine and begins to stifle energy and innovation, WESTS can challenge the old traditions and create new and better methodologies and solutions.

- WEST *irresponsibility* and *recklessness* can sometimes result in creative growth in others.

  When the ball is dropped or ignored by WESTS, it can often force others to compensate by stretching themselves and inventing new plays.

- WEST *inattentiveness* and *boredom* can sometimes result in creating a sense of mystery when a "hard-to-get" approach is needed.

  When it is important to stay cool and not appear over-anxious or over-interested, WESTS can provide a legitimate distractedness and mystique that is hard to read.

- WEST *impulsiveness* and *eccentricity* can sometimes result in breaking through barriers that inspire needed change.

  When some people get stuck in the process of testing the waters, and then testing them again, WESTS can just dive in and swim with the current.

Understanding the Differences Between WEST-NORTHS and WESTS-SOUTHS

The similarities that *The Personality Compass* shows between the North, East, South and West cultures and the four cultural natures allows easy identification and recognition of people's natural qualities and abilities from within the north, east, south and west compass directions. WEST people have similar characteristics to West cultures, and we can know much more about people who are dominant in the WEST direction if we can also identify their subdominant nature. This is always adjacent on the Personality Compass.

Tony and Joanna: Alike and Different

Tony, a dominant WEST-subdominant NORTH, has most of his qualities in common with West cultures, and the second highest number of qualities in common with North cultures. Joanna, a dominant WEST–subdominant SOUTH, has much in common with Tony because of their shared WEST qualities, and many differences from Tony, too, because of their opposite subdominant natures.

The dominant and subdominant natures can both have a significant impact on the types of tasks that appeal to an individual, as well as on the aptitudes required to achieve quality and excellence at the tasks. Tony, a WEST-NORTH, is flexible, creative, assertive, decisive and fast-paced. Joanna, a WEST-SOUTH, is flexible, creative, friendly, caring and cooperative. They have somewhat differing interests and talents, and are not equally suited to the same job, even though both are dominant WESTS.

WEST-NORTH People

Flexible • Creative • Assertive • Decisive • Fast-paced

WEST-SOUTH People

Flexible • Creative • Friendly • Caring • Cooperative

Recognizing WEST Behaviors

Twenty or more crosses (X) *indicate a strong WEST nature.*

WESTS in general . . .

- [ ] Have a sense of being different, individualistic
- [ ] Show little concern for appearances or protocol
- [ ] Are often late or absent without explanation
- [ ] Wear non-traditional clothing and accessories
- [ ] Do things so quickly they can be accident-prone
- [ ] Exhibit a carefree demeanor
- [ ] Seem easily distracted
- [ ] Exude a high level of energy and enthusiasm
- [ ] Stand out as unique
- [ ] Change topics frequently and unexpectedly
- [ ] Go with the flow
- [ ] Speak when and if they feel like it
- [ ] Pay little attention to what others think
- [ ] Hate having to handle details

- [ ] Find it difficult to sit still
- [ ] See the big picture
- [ ] Juggle numerous tasks at once
- [ ] Rebel against rules
- [ ] Like to do the unexpected
- [ ] Stay cool and flexible
- [ ] Display short-term interest
- [ ] Avoid constraints and commitments
- [ ] Start many projects before finishing one
- [ ] Live spontaneously, on the edge
- [ ] Take pride in being unpredictable
- [ ] Put innovative methods as a top priority
- [ ] Motivate others to enjoy every moment
- [ ] Thrive on stirring up the status quo
- [ ] Can brainstorm a million ideas

- [ ] Adapt easily to change
- [ ] Need excitement, adventure, thrills
- [ ] Ignore nagging and nit-picking
- [ ] Keep a loose, relaxed attitude
- [ ] Value imagination, creativity and fun

Recognizing WEST Children

Typical WEST Children in General . . .

- Like to be outdoors
- Don't mind getting dirty, wet or messy
- Find creative uses for common items
- Show enormous imagination in play
- Can be funny and mischievous
- Jump quickly from one toy to another
- Love to try new challenges
- Need to be able to move and explore
- Change the rules in games
- Like the creative and entertaining aspects of school

There was a special twinkle in Suzie's eyes. Somehow, she just looked imaginative. You could almost see the wheels turning in her head, as she thought of tricks to play on the unsuspecting, or antics that might produce a laugh from someone watching her. She loved water colors, and took great pleasure in painting lavender skies with a fuchsia sun. In seventh grade she won a prize at the science fair by actually inventing a better mousetrap. There seemed to be no limit to Suzie's imagination.

Extreme WEST Children in General . . .

- Are under some degree of stress
- Have a knack for getting into trouble
- Do what they want, regardless of rules
- Put their own spin on the truth
- Push their luck to the limit
- Create chaos and confusion for fun
- Lose things frequently
- Take reckless chances at times
- Can have a warped sense of humor
- Display little regard for commitment

Kevin wasn't a bad boy; he just had that reputation. Parents didn't want their children to play with him because, wherever Kevin was, someone always seemed either to get hurt or get into trouble. It was impossible to predict what he might think of and try on a whim, and he couldn't be trusted to do (or not do) what he promised. He seemed to have acceptable intentions, but something would just go wrong somehow. In class, teachers and students alike found him disruptive, even though he often got a laugh.

Recognizing WESTS in Different Roles

As Students
WESTS in General . . .

- Look out the window and daydream a lot
- Go to the pencil sharpener frequently
- Find any excuse to leave the classroom
- Turn in sloppy papers, no matter how brilliant
- Come up with the most and best ideas
- Like to "doodle" as they try to listen
- Have trouble paying attention
- Take risks by talking and passing notes
- Enjoy being the class clown
- Feel rules are made for breaking or at least ignoring
- Show enormous creativity and energy
- May cut classes on nice days

As Athletes
WESTS in General . . .

- Like to play the game, win or lose
- Lack discipline for staying in top shape
- Exhibit fearless gutsiness
- Hate the routine and structure of practice
- Are great at adapting to the unexpected
- Disregard the game plan at times
- Can create exciting, new strategies effortlessly
- Put mistakes or losses behind them quickly
- Play for fun (really!)
- Motivate their teammates to loosen up and relax
- Have a sense of humor about their performance
- May not live up to their potential (but won't mind)

As Leaders
WESTS in General . . .

- Employ a free-rein leadership style
- Are creative visionaries for the future
- Will take the needed risks to reach goals
- Delegate tasks well, but lack follow-up
- Encourage an informal, unstructured atmosphere
- Hold casual meetings and often start late
- Can allow discussions to get off track
- Avoid agendas and minutes when possible
- Find following parliamentary procedure a bore
- May be disorganized and unfocused
- Change direction and policy frequently
- Introduce innovative methods and new ideas

As Friends, Spouses or Parents
WESTS in General . . .

- Are optimistic and encourage optimism in others
- Accept people as they are, and expect the same
- Find creative solutions to problems or obstacles
- Love surprises and change
- Enjoy having a good time even in difficult circumstances
- Carry an aura of excitement wherever they go
- May make promises they don't feel they have to keep
- Exhibit a sense of unpredictability
- Can change their mind without warning
- Have limitless energy for adventure and fun
- Interpret the facts their own way
- Inspire others to soar and follow their dreams

223

Recognizing WESTS in Different Situations

At Home
WESTS in General . . .
- Are not embarrassed by messes
- Spend time playing with their children
- Forget to set the alarm clock
- Spread their projects or hobbies everywhere
- Have an open door policy for drop-ins
- May drive "old jalopies"
- Get involved in numerous clubs and activities that interest them
- Let their children have a lot of freedom
- Mow the grass when they feel like it
- Take little notice of what their neighbors do or think
- Set no schedule for meals or bedtime
- Will have "kid art" and memos everywhere

In a Social Environment
WESTS in General . . .
- Are the life of the party
- Favor the unexpected, the curious, the adventurous
- Enjoy performing or entertaining an audience
- Seek out the most uniquely interesting people
- Will try all types of unusual foods or activities
- May initiate participatory games
- Like to host creative theme parties
- Prefer large groups to an intimate setting
- Take pleasure in casual, outdoor events
- Mix a potpourri of people together well
- Can turn any event into a party
- Get a kick out of wearing costumes or wild outfits

During an Interview
WESTS in General . . .

- May be late and not offer a reason
- Show natural curiosity by distracted eye contact
- Shake hands energetically or not at all
- Explore the surroundings before sitting down
- Ramble from one topic to another
- Have trouble answering questions directly
- Show interest in creative opportunities
- Will not be "dressed to the nines"
- Ask about methods of doing things
- Talk about their innovative ideas
- Appear loose and relaxed, even slouched
- May throw the interviewer off track with the unexpected

On the Job
WESTS in General . . .

- Work best when given freedom and flexibility
- Prefer starting new projects to finishing them
- Avoid detailed paperwork when possible
- Can handle many jobs at once
- Perform tasks in unstructured sequence
- Invent new ways of doing things
- Need opportunities to be creative
- Motivate others by their own enthusiasm
- Are innovative problem-solvers
- Have original, unusual ideas
- Enjoy taking risks and creating excitement
- Love to change things just for the sake of change

Common Comments That Recognize Typical WESTS

"Leopold Bradford's architectural designs are amazing. I've never seen anything like them anywhere. They seem to defy gravity in the way he uses angles, weight and space in unexpected, unpredictable ways. Even though I wouldn't describe his buildings as beautiful, they certainly are interesting and unique. No one could ever accuse him of being a copycat designer; in fact, more and more architects seem to be borrowing rather freely from Bradford's ideas."

Gunther C.

"Adrienne never ceases to surprise me. I knew she was quite a talented painter and sculptress, but I had no idea that she is also a published author, a gourmet cook and an accomplished pianist. One wonders where she finds the time and energy to develop so many talents and skills, but, then, she says she actually hates to take time out to sleep each day. I guess that mind-set explains it."

Alice E.

"Wesley is one of the best newspaper men in the country. His vision twenty years ago turned the sagging sales of his paper around and put it back on top. How he knew what the trends were going to be, I'll never understand. But he was right on target. He seemed to sense when changes were needed, and he was flexible enough to make them before anyone else dared. Not only does he have nerves of steel, but I think he actually enjoys taking big chances."

Everett S.

Common Comments That Recognize Extreme WESTS

"When J. J. rides her Harley, she refuses to wear a helmet. When she goes mountain climbing, she chooses the highest peaks and sheerest cliffs to conquer. She scuba dives in the reefs and goes exploring caves without ropes. She says she enjoys death-defying challenges, but I think she has some kind of morbid death wish."

Tina B.

"Even as a child, Judy was rebellious. If you said go right, she would go left. She was always easy to recognize by the dirt on her face, or the rip in her jeans, while the other girls spent hours on their hair and makeup and planning their perfect wardrobe. Her parents and teachers were always concerned because they could see her potential for a successful future, but Judy only seemed interested in enjoying the moment."

Ruth D.

"No matter how hard he tried, Oliver just didn't seem to fit in with the in-crowd. In grade school, his clothes and shoes and hair – and even his book bags – were never quite in style with the times. In college, he started hanging out with an artsy group that wore really bizarre outfits and dyed their hair bright colors to show their disregard for the socially accepted 'norm'. His excuse for not achieving his dreams became his distaste for having to play by establishment rules."

Jon W.

Motivating WESTS for Success

Tell WESTS that a new, improved method is needed, and they will jump at the opportunity to invent it. Tell them you admire and respect their versatility and creativity, and they will amaze you with their ability to do a dozen different tasks at once, and find six dozen different ways to do them. Tell them you need their great ideas, and WESTS will provide a vision of so many unlimited possibilities, and with such energetic enthusiasm, that you will be drawn into their dreams right along with them. Tell WESTS that they will have the freedom to pull out all the stops and do things their way, and there is no doubt they will produce ingenious results.

What "Turns On" WESTS

- Freedom
- Flexibility
- Few rules
- Imagination
- Unpredictability
- Casual looseness
- Adventurous thrills
- Experimentation

- Brainstorming ideas
- Little structure
- Innovation
- Open-mindedness
- Having fun
- Relaxed atmosphere
- Free-rein leadership
- Constant change

- Enthusiasm
- Creativity
- Individuality
- Visionaries
- Adaptability
- Spontaneity
- Excitement
- Taking risks

Disclosing WEST Pet Peeves

WESTS are turned off by anything which they perceive as boring or ordinary. They have little tolerance for tedious details or the status quo, particularly when either slows down or impedes progress, growth or the creative process. It is best not to inhibit WESTS with a lot of restrictions, because they will rebel and break the rules anyway. Give WESTS plenty of freedom and leeway, and provide ample opportunities for their inventive nature to fly solo. Never insist that there is only one answer, one option, or one perspective – their brain best comprehends multiples, and will rarely be able to reduce infinity to a single common denominator.

What "Turns Off" WESTS

- Narrow-mindedness
- Routine
- Structure
- Nit-picking
- Schedules
- Immobility
- Constraints
- Stagnation
- Repetition
- Required protocol
- Confinement
- Boredom
- Exact expectations
- Rules
- Tedium
- Tunnel vision
- Lists
- Details
- Formality
- Slow pace

Igniting WESTS

WESTS Are Excited By . . .

- New ideas and methodologies
- Interesting people who like to "go for the gusto"
- Variety in day-to-day tasks and projects
- Opportunities to explore many different options
- Creative and innovative thinking
- Freedom to do things when they feel like it
- Thrills and challenges that push their limits
- Coordinating many activities at the same time
- Spontaneity and flexibility for quick changes
- Busy, chaotic, active, even noisy surroundings

WESTS Love To . . .

- Find new ways to solve problems
- Do a task once and forget about it
- Work fast and not worry about perfection
- Ignore rules and policies they disagree with
- Avoid decisions and commitments when possible
- Challenge accepted standards and procedures
- Surprise people with the unexpected
- Be creatively different, not practical
- Use their imagination and inventive ideas
- Live and work in an unstructured environment

Rewarding WESTS

Listed below are a variety of things that WESTS find rewarding. They can be used at home or at work as reinforcers to strengthen WEST performances.

- Implementing their creative ideas
- Unique inventions and gadgets
- Avant-garde pieces of artwork
- Freedom to choose tasks that interest them
- Release from heavy leadership responsibilities
- Tickets to a musical, comedy or concert
- A casual surprise party
- Humorous gag gifts
- Fun clothing with favorite logos
- Sports equipment of their choice
- Flexible work hours
- Excursions or vacations to exciting places
- Opportunities for new and interesting experiences
- Permission to cut down on detailed paperwork
- Puzzles of all kinds
- Games that require group participation
- Do-it-yourself slot or pinball machines
- Pets
- A four-day weekend
- Comfortable and original accessories

Cushioning Clashes with WESTS

When different people, ideas or things make contact and create friction or conflict a clash occurs. The greater the difference, the greater is the conflict. Many clashes among people are caused by differences in priorities. Remember:

- GOALS are naturally important to NORTHS
- FACTS are naturally important to EASTS
- VALUES are naturally important to SOUTHS
- METHODS are naturally important to WESTS

People clash most often over that which is naturally most important to them. Two or more WESTS might clash over differing methods. WESTS and NORTHS might clash when methods conflict with goals. WESTS and EASTS might clash when methods conflict with facts, and WESTS and SOUTHS might clash when methods conflict with values.

Natural Clashes Between Opposites

WESTS	vs	EASTS
Idea-centered	vs	Fact-centered
Innovative	vs	Traditional
Changeable	vs	Structured
Free-rein leaders	vs	Tight-rein leaders
Liberal risk-takers	vs	Conservative planners
Creative visionaries	vs	Analytical pragmatists
Rule breakers	vs	Rule followers
Fast-paced/flexible	vs	Slow-paced/sequential

How to Avoid Conflict with WESTS

- Try new methods
- Don't be narrow-minded
- Stay loose
- Give them freedom
- Value their ideas
- Minimize repetition
- Provide alternatives
- Give them a long leash
- Show flexibility
- Explore
- Seek thrills

- See many solutions
- Take a chance
- Welcome change
- Don't nit-pick
- Be inventive
- Overlook details
- Accept chaos
- Have high energy
- Let them fly
- Share their dreams

- Be imaginative
- Have fun
- Display curiosity
- Show creativity
- Avoid boredom
- Enjoy frivolity
- Aim for the unique
- Be enthusiastic
- Joke around
- Go for it
- Be adventurous

Do's and Don'ts of Living or Working with WESTS

Do's

- Do – be sensitive to WESTS' ideas
- Do – appreciate the WEST need for flexibility
- Do – help WESTS feel energized and motivated
- Do – compliment WESTS' creativity and vision
- Do – recognize WESTS' inventiveness
- Do – encourage WESTS to stay focused
- Do – give WESTS freedom to do their own thing
- Do – take time to help WESTS tie up loose ends
- Do – show tolerance for WESTS' restlessness
- Do – keep up with WESTS' need for frequent change

Give WESTS what they need

The first thing Yolanda did when she entered her new office was rearrange the furniture so that she could look out the window from her desk. She covered her walls with colorful wall hangings and interesting paintings, added unusual sculptures and handpainted bowls among her shelved books, and scattered plants and throw rugs all around. What she loved most about this job was that her boss said she could work from nine to six, instead of eight to five, in order to take her son to school and then pick him up after his hockey practice.

- Don't – let WESTS keep you waiting
- Don't – expect organized tidiness from WESTS
- Don't – be overly protective of WESTS
- Don't – allow WESTS to take dangerous risks
- Don't – openly dare WESTS (they'll do it!)
- Don't – complain about change around WESTS
- Don't – show undue caution or hesitation
- Don't – fight with WESTS – have a sense of humor
- Don't – dawdle on one topic or project too long
- Don't – ask WESTS to follow structured schedules

Don't Try to Tame Wild-Wild WESTS

Commitment was hard for Drew. It wasn't that he feared love, but he feared being trapped into a routine of having every day the same, of feeling obligated to do what someone else expected of him, instead of stepping to the beat of his own drum. Maybe that is why he finally found himself thinking about marriage with Marianna. She didn't try to change him. She actually encouraged him to climb his mountains, and race his dirt bike, and travel to the most challenging ski slopes around the world. When she could join him, she did – and when she couldn't, she didn't try to hold him back. Maybe, at last, this could really work out.

"Best Bets" for Compatibility with WESTS

Take note spouses, children, friends, bosses and co-workers of WESTS! A quick compatibility check will help you identify those who tend to get along best with WEST people.

Personality types that are adjacent to WEST on the Personality Compass (NORTH and SOUTH) are naturally most compatible with WESTS. The highest degree of compatibility usually occurs when both the dominant and subdominant natures are adjacent on the Compass, as illustrated below.

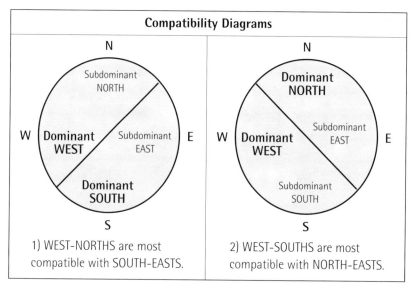

Compatibility Diagrams

1) WEST-NORTHS are most compatible with SOUTH-EASTS.

2) WEST-SOUTHS are most compatible with NORTH-EASTS.

"Cash In" on Compatibility with WESTS

1) WEST-NORTHS and SOUTH-EASTS complement each other by completing the circle of qualities and talents that create well-rounded individuals and teams.

2) WEST-SOUTHS and NORTH-EASTS also function productively because their natures are different, but not opposite, so they enrich each other.

WESTS are not generally compatible with dominant EASTS because they are opposite in nature and have very little in common, unless both types are very well-rounded individuals.

WESTS are usually compatible with other dominant WESTS because they have similar interests and qualities, but they need other types to help them achieve their fullest potential.

Tips for WESTS to Get Along with Others

Directions: WESTS, cross (X) off as you conquer each skill.

☐ Focus on the issue at hand

☐ Value important and helpful details

☐ Plan ahead

☐ Avoid being disorganized and messy

☐ Dress appropriately

☐ Do what you say you will do

☐ Aim for quality, error-free workmanship

☐ Develop a more serious work ethic

☐ Move logically from one subject to another

☐ Finish what you start

☐ Follow through to turn your dreams into realities

☐ Pay closer attention to the world around you

☐ Adhere to the rules

☐ Appreciate facts, not just creative ideas

☐ Be cheerful without annoying others by overdoing it

☐ Realize that new and different is not always better

☐ Pay closer attention to improve accuracy

☐ Meet accepted standards

☐ Become more structured when needed

☐ Learn to appreciate the mundane as well as the thrilling

☐ Stay away from bizarre and weird extremes

☐ Care more about what others think and feel

☐ Take time to analyze the pros and cons

☐ Avoid change just for the sake of change

☐ Practice acting and looking professional

☐ Commit to expectations and responsibilities

☐ Respect traditions

☐ Try to fit in with "the norm"

☐ Don't take dangerous risks

☐ Settle down and lean on others more

☐ Be practical as well as inventive

☐ Scoff less at the way things are

☐ Follow directions carefully

WESTS, Beware!

When people or events drive you crazy and you find yourself feeling bored, restless, a little too committed to suit your free spirit, and you just want to drop everything and escape, STOP! Many WESTS believe that their "live for the moment" drive for adventure adds excitement to the lives of others as well. However, that behavior may be perceived as lack of responsibility.

Targeting WESTS for the Right Job

Terrific Jobs for WESTS

- Project Coordinator
- Architect
- Developer
- Writer
- Story-boarder
- Liaison
- Artist
- Events Director
- Builder

- Advertiser
- Designer
- Realtor
- Partnership Overseer
- National Headhunter
- Performer/Presenter
- Landscaper
- Activities Leader
- Explorer/Guide

Memory Jogger

You need WESTS on the job when . . .

- You need creative ideas and talents
- You need versatile people who adapt easily
- You need innovative, unconventional thinkers
- You need free-spirited risk-takers
- You need to make or coordinate quick changes

Fine-Tuning for WEST Jobs

Hunter, a dominant WEST-subdominant NORTH, is the perfect advertising executive because he has innovative ideas, great creative flair and vision, and he can work fast to meet deadlines – and he also has the confidence and assertiveness to take charge and convince clients to agree with him.

Patrice is a dominant WEST-subdominant SOUTH nature. She is the perfect real estate salesperson because she loves the flexible scheduling and unstructured lifestyle, and she cares about meeting the needs of her clients, always giving them plenty of time and help in making their decisions.

5 Jobs for WEST–NORTH People (and why)
1 Project Coordinator – juggles many tasks (W), leader (N)
2 Advertiser – innovative (W), competitive (N)
3 Developer – visionary (W), self-starting (N)
4 Performer/Presenter – multi-talented (W), confident (N)
5 Builder – dreamer (W), goal-centered (N)

5 Jobs for WEST–SOUTH People (and why)
1 Writer – free-thinking (W), sensitive (S)
2 Story-boarder – idea-centered (W), communicator (S)
3 Liaison officer – flexible (W), helpful (S)
4 Artist – creative (W), introspective
5 Landscaper – sees many options (W), people pleaser (S)

Why WESTS Make Great Employees

WESTS need to be able to push beyond accepted boundaries and cannot tolerate stagnation or immobility. They may seem to be in their own world, almost unaware of others, when they are busy creating. But then they can quickly change demeanor and become a bright ray of hope in an instant. WESTS can function in the midst of confusion better than anyone. WEST individuals are natural risk-takers, and they are happiest finding improved methods and creating changes that will have a positive impact down the road.

WESTS Can Take on a Crisis

Darla, a WEST coordinator for the new Regional Art Gallery, was to be hosting its Grand Opening in only two hours time. The caterer called with last-minute menu changes, the flowers that arrived were not as nice as the arrangements she'd ordered, and the jazz combo she'd lined up turned into a roving violinist due to a sudden emergency. On top of all that, she ripped a hole in her blouse and didn't have time to go home and change. Nevertheless, she remained calm and made a few fast phone calls to arrange for quick-fix solutions. When the first guests arrived, no one would have believed there had ever been a crisis.

WESTS Love to Dare

Ken, a WEST graphic artist, pushed protocol to the limit with his contemporary line drawing of starving children with protruding bellies for the world hunger campaign. His work was a daring, grim reminder of the horrors of hunger, as well as a not-so-subtle symbol of the unborn children of the future should the situation continue unabated.

WESTS Hate to Play It Safe

Julie, a WEST field reporter for a major news agency, thrived on the risks of traveling throughout the world to capture critical stories. From war-torn battlefields to the depths of dark caverns on a rescue mission, Julie never knew when she arose in the morning what the day might bring. But, then, if she did, she would know it was time to change jobs.

WESTS Can Take the Risk

Zoey had wanted to start her own interior design business for a long time, but her family and friends had always talked her out of it, enumerating all the possible pitfalls. Then, one day, she just decided to go for it. Zoey realized the town was growing, and there were no other interior designers to tap the new businesses and new residents who would soon be needing those services. So she convinced the bank to lend her the money, and she set up her first shop. Ten years later she had expanded to six stores.

Top 3 Interview Questions & Answers That Help Hire WESTS for WEST Jobs

1 "Tell me about yourself."

WESTS generally like to talk about exciting and innovative ideas they have, so they might mention things such as:

- New approaches they have used
- Unique methodologies they have encountered
- Creative solutions to problems they have solved
- Their vision of unlimited possibilities
- Profitable risks they have taken
- The wide spectrum of projects they have worked on
- Changes that could improve everyone's future
- A big picture of the way they see their future

2 "What interested you in our company (or the job in question)?"

WEST interest is often whetted by:

- Innovative thinking and methods
- Freedom to try new ideas
- Creative opportunities
- An unstructured environment
- Flexible schedules and projects
- Being involved in a process of change
- People, products or services with a unique style
- Having a loose dress code

3 "Why *should* we hire you?"

WESTS will often describe their own professional strengths as:

- Having a variety of creative talents
- Being innovative problem-solvers
- Coordinating many projects at once
- Seeing the big picture from numerous perspectives
- Willingness to take a risk
- Ability to work without close supervision (they hate it)
- Appreciating diversity in people and projects
- Enjoying chaos, confusion and fast action

Famous WESTS
(Based on historical perception)

Walt Disney
(Creative)

Leonardo daVinci
(Inventive)

Harry Houdini
(Risk-taker)

Pablo Picasso
(Avant-garde)

Galileo
(Visionary)

Christopher Columbus
(Explorer)

Jaques Cousteau
(Adventurous)

Hans Christian Andersen
(Imaginative)

Implementing The Personality Compass:
If You Are a WEST
(Dominant or Subdominant)

What Is Implementation?

Implementation is simply "putting into action", or using something for a particular purpose. *The Personality Compass* is a resource that simplifies the complexities of human behavior so that you can more easily understand yourself and the people around you. *The Personality Compass* also provides practical implementation exercises for you to use on a daily basis to help you develop and improve the entire gamut of personality traits and aptitudes. You can actually use this handbook for three very specific and useful purposes.

Use *The Personality Compass* to Achieve Results

● Develop a well-rounded balance of qualities and skills in yourself and increase your own self-esteem.

● Become an astute, other-oriented communicator and enrich all of your personal and professional relationships.

● Enhance both the breadth and depth of your competencies and increase your success on the job and in your daily life.

Using the Compass to Improve WESTS

What To Do If You Are a WEST

WESTS must learn to think and act EAST:
- To achieve well-rounded balance
- When communicating with EASTS
- In situations, jobs or tasks that require EAST attributes and skills

Know what's in it for WESTS to think and act EAST:
- You will improve your effectiveness in analyzing
- You will become more productive and efficient
- You will increase your ability to be well-rounded
- You will learn to value and develop your weaknesses
- You will get out of your comfort zone and grow
- You will develop self-esteem and power by accomplishing more

Think about the core of the EAST nature:
- EASTS have a logical, factual, analytical nature
- EASTS are cautious, methodical, structured
- EASTS genuinely care about achieving quality
- EASTS love to plan in intricate detail
- EASTS avoid noise and chaos
- EASTS are organized and responsible double-checkers
- EASTS try never to make errors or break protocol

Tips for WESTS on How to Act More EAST

Step 1 Study the EAST sections and Chapter Four of this book.

Step 2 Think of EASTS you know, and ask yourself what they might say or do.

Step 3 Make a concentrated effort to think and act as if you are a dominant EAST.

Step 4 Force yourself to view the world and the people you meet from an EAST perspective.

Step 5 Practice! Practice! Practice! EAST behavior and skills can be learned.

Step 6 Start simply, using the following specific guidelines.

How to Act EAST Step-by-Step

Directions: place a cross (X) *in the blank(s) you need to strengthen, then practice.*

- [ ] Dress conservatively and tastefully
- [ ] Focus your attention without going off on tangents
- [ ] Develop proper posture, poise and manners
- [ ] Avoid sounding silly or illogical, by thinking ahead
- [ ] Stay on task until you finish what you start
- [ ] Listen carefully and take clear notes
- [ ] Be punctual and prepared at all times
- [ ] Put things neatly where they belong
- [ ] Make priority lists and check off items as they are done
- [ ] Plan ahead, then make sure you can find and use the plan
- [ ] Check and double-check everything for accuracy
- [ ] Become more observant of details, or innuendo
- [ ] Organize everything for easy use and access
- [ ] Tune in to cause and effect
- [ ] Follow the rules

Specify What You Need

Evaluation Chart for WESTS

Using the preceding pages as guidelines, list below the behaviors you need to develop first.

Example: _Improved self-presentation_

- _____
- _____

- _____
- _____
- _____

List below a strategy to achieve each of the above.

Example: _Try to envisage the signals my appearance gives to others_

- _____
- _____
- _____
- _____

Identify a EAST person you admire and four characteristics they have that you want/need. Name _____

- _____
- _____

- _____
- _____

Become What You Are Not

Chart For WESTS to Track Your Progress

Directions: Track your behavior improvements in the chart below. Use a cross (X) to indicate status.

Behaviors I have strengthened	Improved in one week	Improved in one month
Watched typical EASTS	☐	☐
Planned ahead	☐	☐
Analyzed	☐	☐
Considered details	☐	☐
Checked for quality	☐	☐
Dressed well	☐	☐
Followed rules	☐	☐
Got organized	☐	☐
Didn't ramble	☐	☐
Was more conservative	☐	☐
Limited some options	☐	☐
Became efficient	☐	☐
Valued accuracy	☐	☐
Played it safe	☐	☐
Became more cautious	☐	☐
Spoke logically	☐	☐

Behaviors I have strengthened	Improved in one week	Improved in one month
Took my time	☐	☐
Sat still	☐	☐
Thought short-term	☐	☐
Focused	☐	☐
Accepted status quo	☐	☐
Concentrated	☐	☐
Measured carefully	☐	☐

Resources I have implemented	Implemented in one week	Implemented in one month
Mentored an EAST	☐	☐
Read about EAST	☐	☐
Observed many EASTS	☐	☐
Learned to value EASTS	☐	☐
Practiced being EAST	☐	☐

Using the Personality Compass to Improve WEST Relationships

Understanding the WEST "Blind Spot"

Stand in one place and hold your head perfectly still, facing straight ahead. Roll your eyes as far to the left and right as possible, and note exactly what lies within your realm of vision. That which lies just beyond what you can see in your peripheral vision is known as your "blind spot". It is there, but you simply can't see it.

Human nature also has "blind spots". You can see things in others that they do not see in themselves – and others can see things in you that you have trouble seeing in yourself. The most common "blind spot" in WESTS, which can cause problems for themselves and others, is putting the need for excitement as a top priority. They don't perceive themselves as thrill-seekers, yet it is at the core of their nature.

WEST Free-Spiritedness Can Hurt Relationships

Max was really getting bored with Sandy's ever-increasing need for them to stay home with the baby. Of course he loved his new son, but did becoming parents automatically mean that he and Sandy should no longer need to go out and enjoy their friends or a good party? And now Sandy was encouraging him to sell his motorcycle and scuba diving equipment to help with the added expenses and to keep him safe so that he will be able to work and accept more responsibilities. Well, no way . . . he will not become a boring couch potato just because he is now a father!

Perception: The Root of Most Problems

Sandy's Perception

● Sandy loves Max and their new son, and she wants to establish a secure family life for all of them.

● Sandy respects Max's need to go out and have fun, and to keep a sense of excitement in his life, but not at the risk of not facing up to his new responsibilities.

● Sandy needs to know that Max will be there for her and their new son, that they can count on him now and in the future.

Max's Perception

● Max loves Sandy and their new son, too; but he values enjoying life's adventures far more than security.

● Max respects Sandy's role as new mother, and understands the protectiveness that she must be

feeling, but he told her from the beginning not to try to force him into the mold of a typical suburban husband.

● Max needs to feel that he can continue to live life the way he enjoys it, without being considered a bad husband or father.

Solutions: Give and Take

- Compromise is at the heart of any solution to a problem.

- Sandy and Max need to communicate about their feelings and needs, and negotiate what each is willing to accept from the other.

- Sandy should gently reveal how Max's need for excitement and his thrill-seeking behavior affects the family.

- Max needs to set aside some quiet family time at home to establish a sense of family security for all of them.

- Sandy needs to accept the qualities in Max that drew her to him in the first place. Deep down, she wouldn't want him to give up the adventures he loves . . . but maybe they can create a few special events in both of their lives to keep the thrill of love alive for the family.

Questions & Answers About the WEST Personality

Question   Why are some WESTS so hard to follow in a conversation, always jumping from one topic to another, without clear transitions of thought?

Answer   *That's how the WEST brain works, thinking of a dozen things at once. They don't need to "connect the dots" to see the whole picture. In fact, because they are not limited by logic and chronology, they have almost an aerial view of reality. Although this characteristic can be confusing in conversation, it can certainly lead to great ideas with a totally unique perspective. To overcome this hurdle when having discussions with WESTS, just ask them to slow down and spell out their point for you – or ask them specific questions that will clarify what they mean.*

Question   Why do some WESTS seem to have a death wish, always needing to challenge fate to the limit by free-falling out of planes, scaling vertical cliffs, racing motorcycles at top speed and other death-defying feats?

Answer   *Recent evidence indicates that at least part of the reason may be related to an elongated gene known as D4DR, which helps regulate the chemical messenger, dopamine, in the brain. There is little doubt that WEST personality types have at least some form of this gene, as well as another four or five dopamine-related genes (and, of course, environment and opportunity are also contributing factors). The*

bottom line is that there are both physiological and social reasons that thrill-seeking WESTS get an adrenalin rush from danger and risk. They can't help it. It is not a matter of being able to control their need to push themselves to the limit at a logical level. They love it, and require it almost like an addiction. The degree of risk needed by WEST individuals seems to be directly related to the amount of dopamine produced by the body and the kind of upbringing they experience.

Question **Why do some WESTS have a tendency to start several projects at once, and then leave the unfinished mess and chaos they created, while they begin even more projects, which they also leave unfinished?**

Answer *WESTS are initiators. They get ideas and they can't wait to try them out. However, they get bored very easily, so they work on something for a little while and then they want to move on to something new. Their quest for that which is exciting and interesting, and their need for constant change, makes it difficult for WESTS to focus on one thing at a time and follow it through to the finish. Nagging will not be effective with WESTS, so offer them incentives that will motivate them to finish what they start and to clean up their mess. At any rate, give WESTS plenty of freedom to explore with their creative energy (always within reasonable constraints, of course), because out of their chaos can often come sparkles of brilliance.*

Chapter Seven

People Aren't Difficult...
Just Different

Differences Can Be Valuable

When we first started this book, we knew we were different (Diane is an EN-S, while Thelma is a SW-E) but we had no idea how to use that knowledge of ourselves and each other to make our lives more peaceful and more productive. We nearly drove each other crazy before we figured it out.

For example, in our early drafts of *The Personality Compass*, we would brainstorm our ideas together, then Diane would commit the words to paper and Thelma would enter the copy into the computer and return it to Diane for editing. Without fail, Thelma's first computer copy would come back to Diane with nine or ten errors. Diane would almost gleefully encircle Thelma's mistakes with a bright red pen and return them to her for corrections. The second and third and fourth computer drafts would still have errors, and Diane would explode in frustration at having to waste time proofing the same page half a dozen times. Thelma would feel hurt and incompetent at her inability to catch her mistakes each time. Of course, most of the ideas that emerged on the page had come from Thelma's creativity, even though it was Diane's language skills that put the ideas into words. Finally, Diane put a fat, green pen in Thelma's hand and told her to mark through every red mark as soon as she made that correction in the computer. Thelma was asked not to give Diane a print-out until every correction was made and checked off with her green pen.

As simple as it sounds, that single strategy probably saved our relationship and the book. Thelma was able to "do it right the first time", which is an important time-saver for Diane's EAST-NORTH nature. In return, Diane learned to take a few deep breaths and not to get upset when Thelma's SOUTH-WEST would come up with a way to make the page easier and better for the reader a week later, and want to change it. We mentored with each other to achieve the balance we needed in all four dimensions to increase our individual and team competence and to improve our relationship.

Understanding the need to value each other's strengths was the first step, but actually finding ways to develop the strengths and skills that were difficult for our individual natures is what saved the project and the partnership. Using and implementing what we learned about ourselves and each other made the critical difference in our ability to work as a team to achieve our goal – publication!

Differences Can Enhance Teams
Even though most of us value qualities and abilities that are similar to those we possess ourselves, few of us would fail to recognize the value of differences in most outstanding teams. Consider the need for different skills in the following different types of successful teams.

- Contract teams for laying the Alaskan Pipeline – Alaska (N)
- The Toyota Corporation – Japan (E)
- Reggae steel drum bands – The Caribbean (S)
- Olympic women's ice hockey – USA (W)

Distinguishing Differences

In Image...

NORTHS	reflect	Achievement
EASTS	reflect	Quality
SOUTHS	reflect	Compassion
WESTS	reflect	Originality

In Attitudes...

NORTHS call a spade a spade

EASTS call a spade by its precise scientific name

SOUTHS call a spade whatever it wants to be called

WESTS don't want to limit a spade by assigning a name to it

In Priorities...

GOALS are most important to **NORTHS**

Example: doing whatever it takes to finish tasks and meet deadlines.

FACTS are most important to **EASTS**

Example: getting correct information to fulfill exact requirements.

VALUES are most important to **SOUTHS**

Example: exemplifying loyalty, trust and cooperation with others.

METHODS are most important to **WESTS**

Example: finding innovative ways to adapt to change and solve problems.

Differences Can Create Difficulties

Characteristics of Differences
- Unique, distinct
- Recognizably not the same
- Distinguishable
- Diverse, unlike
- Separate, varied

Characteristics of Difficulties
- Disagreeable, troublesome
- Hard to understand
- Hard to deal with
- Not easy, hard to read
- Puzzling, laborious

Valuing Differences Ends Fingerpointing

Differences are often perceived as difficulties. When asked to describe a difficult person, most people will describe someone who is exactly the opposite of their own nature. For example, most NORTHS will describe SOUTH qualities as difficult, EASTS will find WEST traits offensive, SOUTHS will mention their discomfort with NORTH behaviors, and WESTS will often talk about the way EAST characteristics get on their nerves.

In short, opposite natures and personalities are natural nemeses to each other. Understanding the inherently different priorities, perceptions, value systems and behavior patterns among the four different natures can help us stop fingerpointing and see that the people most of us think of as difficult, are really only different from us. This enlightened perspective, based on viewing the profound complexities of human nature in the simplest, most basic terms, is the first step toward creating the kind of understanding that can inspire greater harmony among all types of people in all types of cultures.

Perception Differences at a Glance

Perception is the ultimate reality

NORTH Perception of NORTHS	EAST Perception of NORTHS	SOUTH Perception of NORTHS	WEST Perception of NORTHS
Capable Decisive	Controlling Arrogant	Intimidating Bossy	Driven Demanding
NORTH Perception of EASTS	**EAST Perception of EASTS**	**SOUTH Perception of EASTS**	**WEST Perception of EASTS**
Picky Inflexible	Reliable Competent	Tedious Snobbish	Uptight Obsessive
NORTH Perception of SOUTHS	**EAST Perception of SOUTHS**	**SOUTH Perception of SOUTHS**	**WEST Perception of SOUTHS**
Slow Vulnerable	Emotional Chatty	Warm Caring	Dependent Helpless
NORTH Perception of WESTS	**EAST Perception of WESTS**	**SOUTH Perception of WESTS**	**WEST Perception of WESTS**
Undependable Noncommital	Careless Disorganized	Defiant Rebellious	Fun Interesting

Similarities That Create Cohesion

NORTHS & EASTS	Work hard	Are productive	Take responsibility	Are serious	Finish tasks	Catch mistakes

NORTHS & WESTS	Move fast	Are talkative	Enjoy action	Welcome change	Are bold	Take risks

SOUTHS & EASTS	Move slowly	Listen well	Are conservative	Avoid change	Are cautious	Follow rules

SOUTHS & WESTS	Motivate others	Are sociable	Shun deadlines	Are adaptable	Avoid pressure	Enjoy relaxation

Note: opposite natures are not similar

When Extreme Behaviors Become Difficult

NORTHS might be perceived as difficult if they . . .

- Blow-up easily
- Won't listen to others' points of view
- Embarrass others publicly
- Perceive suggestions as complaints
- Are insensitive to others' feelings
- Believe they are always right
- Have an uncooperative attitude
- Seek personal gain
- Need to have control
- Are intimidating
- Don't respect authority
- Are arrogant

EASTS might be perceived as difficult if they . . .

- Nit-pick over every detail
- Can only do one thing at a time
- Refuse to change old habits
- Give long, tedious explanations
- Isolate themselves from others
- Require absolute perfection
- See only one perspective/solution
- Lack a sense of humor
- Need to follow a rigid routine
- Are cautious to a fault
- Analyze things to death
- Require everything in writing

Note: low self-esteem, exhaustion or stress can lead to extreme behaviors

SOUTHS might be perceived as difficult if they . . .

- Need to be prodded to work
- Have to be told what to do and how
- Deny that problems exist
- Paint rose-colored pictures of the facts
- Are slow to grasp job expectations
- Lack motivation to excel
- Talk behind people's backs
- Complain without solutions
- Avoid confrontation/problems
- Get feelings hurt easily
- Won't speak up and speak out
- Are painfully slow and late

WESTS might be perceived as difficult if they . . .

- Don't give explicit information
- Have an "I don't care" attitude
- Lack pride in their work
- Expect others to read their minds
- Won't commit anything to writing
- Think horseplay is funny
- Are indifferent to responsibilities
- Make a lot of mistakes
- Won't conform to proper protocol
- Rebel against rules and structure
- Are insensitive to time
- Need to change everything

Note: low self-esteem, exhaustion or stress can lead to extreme behaviors

Diffusing Difficulties

Tips to Diffuse Difficulties with NORTHS

1 Stand up, look directly in the eye, and use a firm, not hostile, voice.
2 Listen to what they say, only if they remain calm and respectful.
3 If they interrupt you or lose their temper, tell them you will discuss this when they are willing to treat you with respect, and walk away.
4 Insist that they listen to your point of view and tell them that you will not be manipulated – but never give them excuses.

Tips to Diffuse Difficulties with EASTS

1 Pay close attention to what they say (you might even take notes).
2 Tell them you understand their position or criticism, point out the other facts / perspectives to be considered and give your point of view.
3 Build a logical, persuasive argument to rebut their position or criticism – or agree openly with them – based only on the evidence.
4 If they get bogged down in details, usurping your time, tell them to put it in writing, leave and respond ASAP in writing.

Tips to Diffuse Difficulties with SOUTHS

1 Give a friendly smile, handshake, or pat on the back, and chat with them informally for a few minutes.

2 Listen to them so long as the conversation remains relevant (you may have to gently interrupt them to keep them on track).

3 Show understanding for their feelings, but point out that they may be making a mountain out of a molehill, and why.

4 Talk in a kind way, explain how you see the problem, guide them to find their own solutions – then get off the subject of problems.

Tips to Diffuse Difficulties with WESTS

1 In an environment with few distractions ask for their full attention.

2 Show a sense of humor and adopt a casual, informal demeanor.

3 Ask specific questions so they tell you what you need to know.

4 Be open-minded to their ideas, no matter how bizarre – then focus them on the one or two you like and let them run with those.

Learning to Value All Four Types

How You Learn Determines What You Value

(. . . and what you value determines how you learn)

NORTHS
- Learn by
  "Doing"
- Value **Action**

WESTS
- Learn by
  "Experimenting"
- Value **Discovery**

EASTS
- Learn by
  "Analyzing"
- Value **Logic**

SOUTHS
- Learn by
  "Listening"
- Value **People**

Never expect your children, friends or co-workers to learn the same way you do.
Present learning opportunities that target a person's values for best results.
Because of differing values, it is interesting to note that . . .

- NORTHS Get the Job Done Fast
- EASTS Do It Right the First Time
- SOUTHS Build the Best Teams
- WESTS Expand All Horizons

What You Value Determines What You Contribute Best

(... and what you contribute best is determined by what you value)

NORTHS
naturally contribute
best to the
Work Force

WESTS
naturally contribute
best to the
The Arts/Invention

EASTS
naturally contribute
best to the
World of Intellect

SOUTHS
naturally contribute
best to the
Relaitionships

The more balanced you become in all four natures, the more personally and professionally successful you will be, and the more contributions you will make to your family, your job, your community and your world. Whatever people contribute, it is interesting to note that ...

- NORTHS Do It with Confidence
- EASTS Do It with Class
- SOUTHS Do It with Feeling
- WESTS Do It with Imagination

Becoming Your Personal and Professional Best

NORTHS need to develop the SOUTH strengths of:

- Friendliness and warmth
- Good listening skills
- Patience and understanding
- Kind helpfulness
- Spreading goodwill
- Being a team player

EASTS need to develop the WEST strengths of:

- Open-mindedness
- Energetic enthusiasm
- Seeing many alternatives
- Creative ideas
- Adaptability to change
- Worry-free attitude

SOUTHS need to develop the NORTH strengths of:

- Decisiveness
- Self-confidence
- Taking initiative
- Finding pleasure in work
- Finishing tasks on time
- Assertiveness

WESTS need to develop the EAST strengths of:

- Planning for best results
- Logical thinking
- Doing it right the first time
- Achieving quality
- Organizational skills
- Reliability

You Need Each Other

NORTHS Need SOUTH Qualities and Skills

Tyler, a NORTH Manager, was called aside by the new Chief Executive. "You're a talented leader," he was told, "and you always meet our weekly quotas. The one area that you might want to work on is what we call people skills. Just be a little more friendly with the customers, and encourage your department to work together as a team to keep the shelves filled and straightened."

EASTS Need WEST Qualities and Skills

Debra, an EAST cashier, was excellent at ringing the merchandise according to the correct code without fail. However, she became very irritable when customers changed their mind and decided not to purchase an item she had already rung up, or added a last-minute item. Her merit review was perfect, with the exception of one sentence: "Develop more flexibility when handling the unexpected demands of dealing with the public."

SOUTHS Need NORTH Qualities and Skills

Scott, a SOUTH insurance agent, loved his job because he knew he was truly helping people to protect themselves for the future. He enjoyed meeting new people and spending time with them in their offices and homes as he helped them meet their particular insurance needs. But he knew that in order to get the coveted Salesman of the Year Award he was going to have to improve his ability to turn his reports in on time to meet the critical deadlines that determine the beginning date of policy coverage.

WESTS Need EAST Qualities and Skills

Pierre, a WEST hair stylist, won numerous awards for his unique designs and creations on several continents. Luckily for him he had a reliable assistant who made sure that everything he needed was always at his fingertips and in excellent repair, because Pierre was oblivious to the mundane tasks required to make his art possible. It never occurred to him that detailed planning and effort went into preparing for his success. All he had to do was to show up and create.

Balance Creates Success

By Developing Your Own NORTH Strengths, You Can...

- Complete a billion dollar project ahead of schedule
- Lead the biggest fundraiser in history
- Coach a mediocre team to the championship
- Turn a farthing into a fortune
- Be the first person to jump into action
- Find the best way to outwit an adversary
- Beat impossible odds to achieve a goal
- Negotiate the toughest contract with confidence
- Surprise friends with reservations at the best restaurant
- Run the shortest, most purposeful meetings ever held

By Developing Your Own EAST Strengths, You Can...

- Organize the classiest events on record
- Find the needle in the haystack
- Rescue sub-standard products from delivery
- Develop fail-safe systems that ensure quality
- Work around the clock to find an error
- Relay perfect, detailed messages
- Keep the best files and records in the company
- Chair the most organized meetings ever attended
- Be the most efficient and mannerly person around
- Give directions that anyone can follow

By Developing Your Own SOUTH Strengths, You Can...

- Be the first person to volunteer for service, or to help
- Build a cohesive team of loyal players
- Shine during the process of communication with people
- Listen more attentively than anyone in the world
- Be the perfectly charming diplomat in any situation
- Act as peace-maker in the midst of conflict
- Receive top honors in salesmanship
- Stand out as the nicest, friendliest person in the crowd
- Choose right over wrong
- Instruct others with patience

By Developing Your Own WEST Strengths, You Can...

- Invent a better mousetrap
- Throw the most unusual parties imaginable
- Motivate large groups of people to get involved
- Contribute the most and best ideas of anyone
- Coordinate several big projects simultaneously
- Develop innovative solutions to common problems
- Find new methods for improving the status quo
- Hold the most creative meetings ever experienced
- See beyond the way things are, to the possibilities
- Take the risk needed to get off "square one"

Steps for Success Using The Personality Compass

1 Become other-oriented when communicating with people for best results. Here's how:

    A Use your knowledge of the Compass to determine the person's probable dominant nature.

    B Put your own dominant nature aside, for the moment, and communicate according to the nature of the person with whom you are relating. (Example: Even if you happen to be a NORTH, it is imperative that you deal with SOUTHS with SOUTH behavior on your part, and use EAST behaviors with EASTS, WEST behaviors with WESTS, etc).

2 Develop the skills and behaviors from all four personality types on *The Personality Compass*, to the very best of your ability, regardless of your own nature. Follow these simple steps:

    A Force yourself, if necessary, to recognize the value of all four natures and the natural skills and qualities that make each uniquely effective and valuable in certain situations or jobs, or in particular relationships.

    B Observe and mentor with people who are different from you so that you can become a more well-rounded, skilled and compatible individual.

    C Practice your weakest skills and qualities until they become genuine personal strengths for you, regardless of your inherent nature.

3 Work continuously on taming the more extreme characteristics of your nature, where appropriate. These tips will help:

A   Be honest with yourself about your possible shortcomings.
B   Appreciate your good qualities and strengths, and recognize the advantages to improving yourself so that you can maintain respect from others and a high regard for yourself, because high self-esteem is critical for healthy relationships and career success.
C   Think before you speak or act in order to stay in control of your behavior at all times, remembering that typical other-oriented communication is generally the most effective and successful.

Getting in touch with yourself and the people who impact your life is a learning process that can take a lifetime. *The Personality Compass* can shorten your journey and lighten your load so that you can reach your destination faster. It is critical that every person learns to value and develop the diverse qualities and talents of all four cultures and personality types. Relationships will improve. Self-esteem will soar. Career success will increase. Perhaps the most important message of *The Personality Compass* is that we all need each other to complete our best selves.

Using the Personality Compass in Real Life

Letter from a Lover

"We were able to end the relationship lovingly…"

. . . It is my firm belief that *The Personality Compass* has just saved me from a life of misery with the wrong man (and saved him from the wrong woman as well). I am a WEST-NORTH and Brandon is an EAST-SOUTH. At first, I think our opposite natures attracted us to one another. I take pride in being a fun-loving free spirit, always ready for a new and exciting adventure. I like parties and crowds, loud music, dancing and keeping busy so that I am not bored. Never could I take a desk job that requires sitting at a computer all day. I've been a bartender, a white-water rafting guide, and am presently Manager of the Art Nouveau Museum.

Brandon is really a terrific guy – handsome, well-dressed and neat. He is generous, thoughtful and very romantic. His attentiveness and willingness to try things I enjoy swept me off my feet. He focused on me and was sensitive to my feelings and needs. But he also had a moody and quiet side. In time, I began to feel that he was judging me with disapproval, although he never openly criticized me. I eventually felt that I somehow needed to squelch my natural flamboyance and energy. I guess I felt that I embarrassed him. At first he took me to the best restaurants and concerts, and then we began to spend more and more time staying in, instead of going out. It didn't take me long to become bored and for him to become suspicious – a deadly combination.

So, who is right and who is wrong in this situation? Through *The Personality Compass* we were both able to see that we are both right – just very different. It was a relief to be able to end the relationship lovingly, without guilt or blame, and with our self-esteem intact. *The Personality Compass* helped us do that. Thank you!

Nancy N.

Winning at Work

"I finally got that promotion . . ."

. . . I can't tell you how grateful I am to you and to *The Personality Compass* . . . I finally got that promotion at work that passed me by for the last two years, and felt compelled to tell you.

It was amazing! After realizing that my boss is a NORTH-EAST, I was able to see why my SOUTH-WEST personality was driving him crazy. I stopped complaining, visiting too long with my co-workers, and coming in late several times a week. Then, I made a conscious effort to speed up my work habits, answer exactly the questions I was asked without digression or embellishment, and proof my reports more carefully to make sure they were error-free before sending him a copy (with the help of one of my EAST friends at work – mentoring is a great tool). Of course, I'm still working on many other areas of improvement, but these were causing me the most trouble on the job.

Success at last! *The Personality Compass* analogy makes sense. If I have a problem trying to remember what a NORTH would like or dislike, I just ask myself what a Viking might want, and the answer becomes quite clear. It's so simple – the *Compass* is great . . .

Chuck A.

Fine-tuning Friendship

"I've wondered why something seems to be missing . . . "

. . . Angie and I have been friends for twenty years, and for twenty years I've wondered why something seems to be missing, even though we see each other often. Now I'm beginning to understand.

My NORTH nature needs a strong person who will not be afraid to speak her mind, and who can enter into debates from time to time (about politics, child-rearing, etc) and enjoy a good argument occasionally. Also, I need friends who go for their goals instead of sitting around and making excuses for not being able to achieve their dreams. I just can't tolerate whining and complaining. My philosophy is, "Get up off your butt and do **something**, even if it's wrong!" Angie can't, or won't (she's obviously a SOUTH), and then she mopes about it, which really irritates me.

So, why are we friends? Probably because she totally admires me and looks up to me. I realize now that I've been using her, in a way, to feed my own ego and to encourage me. Our entire relationship has been centered around me. But now, just writing this letter, I realize that I need to help change that. I'm going to focus on meeting her needs for a change. Maybe I can support her and help her fight through her fears. I hope so. In any case, maybe giving something back will fill the void I've been feeling . . .

Lynda V.

Praise from a Parent

"The Compass has helped me build stronger and closer
relationships with my children . . ."

. . . What a treasure *The Personality Compass* provided me by explaining for me why my son is not as good a student in school as my daughter, even though his IQ test results seem quite a bit higher. Being able to understand that Todd's WEST nature naturally rebels against all the rules and structure of most school environments, while Tanya's EAST nature thrives within those constraints, has been a godsend for me. I've been overwhelmed with worry and guilt, and using the *Compass* has released me from all that and helped me to take specific steps to ensure that both Todd and Tanya are given opportunities and resources to learn in ways that are appropriate to their individual natures and personalities. In fact, I have discussed your model with many of their teachers, as well as a few of my friends on the school board . . .

Thank you for the peace of mind that you have given me as a mother. *The Personality Compass* has helped me build stronger and closer relationships with my children, with far less conflict. It's a miracle.

Betsy S.

Yearnings of Youth

"I want to be popular, but nobody likes me..."

. . . All my life I've hated myself because I can be so mean and hateful to people. I scream and yell when I don't get my own way, and this has ruined my life. I want to be popular, but nobody likes me, and I don't blame them – I don't like me either. (I'm sure I'm a NORTH with low self-esteem.)

But *The Personality Compass* has given me hope. I'm really concentrating on learning to be more SOUTH. I've been practicing SOUTH behaviors for about three months now, and the kids at school are already being nicer to me. My best friend is a SOUTH and she helps me. Today two girls asked me to sit with them at lunch. Being friendly and nice pays off, and I've been controlling my anger a lot better by understanding that my way and my feelings are not the only right ones. The *Compass* shows that everyone has good points...

Mia D.

Competing for Control

" I felt like she was running my life…"

… My secretary, Sally, is terrific (she's a NE personality type, without a doubt). She comes in early and stays late when we have critical deadlines to meet. She makes sure that my phone calls are screened and won't allow anyone to interrupt me unnecessarily, and she can type faster than anyone in the building.

So, what was my problem? I felt like she was running my life! I had no control over parts of my own business, and it was even overlapping into my personal life. One day she even told my wife that I couldn't be disturbed! (Sally is happily engaged, so this was not a matter of any hanky-panky going on between us, or jealousy. She just wanted to make sure that I'm protected so that I can do what I need to do as stress-free as possible, but she went too far.)

The Personality Compass made me realize that all difficulties with people can be resolved with a bit of thought and planning. Of course, I didn't want to alienate a great secretary, and I certainly didn't want to ignite her strong temper for fear that she might quit. After re-evaluating the NORTH and EAST characteristics several times, I realized that Sally needed to have a higher degree of control than a non-NORTH secretary, and as a subdominant EAST she would not welcome major changes.

My solution was simple. I had a private line installed in my office, and gave the number only to my family and very closest friends, staff and clients. I did not make that line available for the switchboard or my secretary to answer. That way, I am assured that I will receive all urgent and personal calls myself and Sally is still doing things her way, as she has done for five years.

Henry L.

Pre-teen Perspectives

"My mom used to nag me all the time about everything..."

... I'm twelve years old. My name is Katrina. You probably never received a letter from a kid before, but I wanted to tell you thank you. Since my mom and I have been using your **Compass**, my life has gotten a lot better.

My mom used to nag me all the time about everything. Cleaning my room; doing my homework; picking up my messes before I even made them; and brushing my teeth. She would inspect how I brushed and make me do it over and over until she decided my teeth were perfect. It drove me nuts. I thought mom was crazy until I learned about *The Personality Compass* at our YMCA workshop. I brought it home and showed my whole family, especially Mom.

We had a good time trying to figure out what types we are. Mom is an EAST and I'm a WEST. *The Personality Compass* helped her see how her nagging made me want to scream. She realized she needed to relax a little bit and not demand perfection every second. I still have to do stuff, but Mom isn't so mean about it now. She lets me do it on my own more. I really like the *Compass*.

Katrina J.

288

Happiness at Home

"I'm much happier, so I'm a better wife..."

...If I could give you a big hug, I would! Your *Personality Compass* has changed my life so much! After my husband attended one of your workshops, where you introduced *The Personality Compass*, he has been so different. He is making an effort to try to understand me and my feelings for the first time.

As a SOUTH (yes, he taught me all about the *Compass*, too), I really need for Doug (my WEST husband) to listen to me, and spend time talking with me. He was always dashing around, in a hurry, and leaving me to feel alone and rejected. He's still very busy, but he makes time to have at least one good conversation with me every day, or at least almost every day. I'm much happier, so I'm a better wife, which makes him happy too.

Kelly Z.

Questions & Answers About Using the Personality Compass in Your Daily Life

Question I live in the East, but I am a WEST personality type. What should I do? (I can't move out West.)

Answer *Work on developing more of your EAST qualities. They will come in handy no matter where you live, which is true of all four groups of nature traits. All types of people live in each of the four geographical regions, but strengthening the nature which is analogous to where you live will help you feel more comfortable and be more effective in that cultural environment.*

Question I am a SOUTH personality type, but I am in a job that requires mostly NORTH skills. Should I look for a SOUTH job? (With unemployment so high, I doubt I can afford to be that picky.)

Answer *You would naturally be much more comfortable and more competent in a SOUTH job, so it wouldn't hurt to keep your antennae up in case one comes along. However, you can learn to be more NORTH by watching and mentoring with NORTHS. You can also practice acting NORTH, even though it is against your nature and will be difficult for you at first. All skills can be learned. The degree of competence you achieve in developing the attitudes and strengths of each type depends on your own insight, will, determination and practice.*

Question I am a SOUTH teacher and I truly love my elementary students, but my son has always hated school. Is that my fault? What might I have done to turn him against it?

290

Answer   *Perhaps nothing. It is quite possible that your son simply has a WEST nature, which naturally dislikes and often rebels against rigid structure, rules and exact expectations. Paying careful attention to one topic for precisely forty-two minutes without daydreaming out the window is far easier for an EAST than it is for a WEST.*

Question   **The NORTH traits that I admire most in my husband at work (his strength, decisiveness and leadership) become frightening at home when there's no one around for him to impress (he bullies me, puts down the children, and actually becomes aggressive and violent when he gets angry). How can the same man be so different?**

Answer   *The most admirable characteristics of any of the four nature types can shift from typical to extreme under certain conditions. Long-term extreme behaviors often mean the person has low self-esteem. More short-term extreme behaviors are probably due to stress or exhaustion. Fortunately, all three conditions can be temporary, although turning low self-esteem to high may require professional counseling and take some time.*

Question   **I'm an EAST and that's who I am. I don't want to "Go WEST" or anywhere else on the Personality Compass. I like being an EAST and I don't want to be anything else. People will have to accept me as I am, or just get used to it. Why should I try to change who I am?**

Answer   *You shouldn't try to change who you are – you probably couldn't change your inherent personality type by learning about and* developing the qualities and talents that are natural to the other three types. It is a matter of growing, not changing. You can develop a broader spectrum of skills and competencies from which to choose, based on the need for those abilities in a particular situation, or when dealing with a particular person or group. This kind of growth can increase the chances of your success both in relationships and in your job or career. The first step is learning to value the traits that are different from those that are natural to you – because those are the ones you need most.

Question   **Why do you call the Personality Compass a tool? I see it as an interesting idea, but not really as a tool. What does that mean?**

Answer   ***The Personality Compass*** *is a tool because it is a resource that you can actually use to achieve a specific purpose and get a needed result. First, you need to grasp what it can be used for (to understand yourself and other people better, and to deal more effectively with all types of personalities in all types of situations). Then, you need to understand how to use it (look up what you need to know in the handbook, which is graphically designed as a quick and easy reference guide – then practice doing what the book suggests). As you become more proficient in addressing people and situations according to their needs, rather than according to what is natural and easiest for you, the positive results will prove that* **The Personality Compass** *is a useful tool that works.*

Question   **The concept of four personality types has been around for a long time. Why not just leave it alone, instead of coming up with yet**

another way to label those types?

Answer　*Our global society seems to demand a constant quest for that which is quicker, easier and more practical, especially now. With the worldwide capabilities of the Internet, it has become even more imperative that people are able to communicate effectively at an international level that will take into account an understanding, value, and respect for cultural differences. The Personality Compass addresses the demand by simplifying that which is already accepted in the scientific community and the world at large, while maintaining integrity and accuracy of the established principles. By emphasizing the identification both of one's dominant and subdominant types, the Personality Compass increases the accuracy of typing, and the understanding of each person's nature as unique within the parameters of a universal personality type. In short, the Personality Compass makes the known scientific data more useful for the lay person in everyday life throughout the world.*

Question　**I've been married twice. My first wife and I were not compatible at all, but my second wife and I get along great. I don't think I've changed much, so what does that say about my marriages? Was my first marriage doomed from the start because we were the wrong personality types? If so, a lot of emotional and financial costs could have been saved if there had been a way to predetermine compatibility before our relationship started to develop.**

Answer　*Although the idea seems almost humorous and trite, it is not altogether out of the realm of reason. Of course, few relationships or situations are "doomed from the start" because outcomes often depend upon the wisdom and efforts that are put into them. However, it is true that some people are, by nature, simply not compatible. We know, for example, that people with diametrically opposite natures have very little in common and tend to get on each other's nerves over time, unless both individuals are very well-rounded and balanced in all four directions. The good news is that even strong opposites in a relationship can learn to balance their own natures by developing some of the traits from their opposite type in order to meet the needs of their partner better. Ideally, checking out compatibility in advance through the Personality Compass can help us make more enlightened choices and efforts which can benefit all of our relationships.*

Question   **As publisher of a major newspaper, I need mostly NORTH-WEST employees who can meet deadlines and are also willing to take risks in order to get the big stories. What I've discovered, though, is that I have a lot of SOUTH-EASTS working for me. They undoubtedly came across as charming and competent in their interview – but now what do I do?**

Answer   *There are three solutions to this very common dilemma. One is to transfer any SOUTH-EAST employees that you can to SOUTH-EAST jobs, when and if that is feasible, because you and they will be happier. Another solution is to provide special training for your SOUTH-EAST employees to develop NORTH-WEST qualities and skills. Finally, as positions become available, you can make sure you target and hire the personality type you need for each position. As you seem to be aware, placing the right person in the right job improves efficiency, quality, productivity, motivation and morale. In other words, astute hiring and job placement increases profit dollars.*

Question   **I seem to have an equal number of characteristics from all four personality types. I honestly have no idea which one is dominant or subdominant. I seem to belong right in the middle, so how can I relate to the Personality Compass?**

Answer   *The fact is, no matter how well balanced you are in all four nature types, you will be dominant in one, and subdominant in another that is adjacent to your dominant type on the Compass. Because it is usually easier to identify the nature that is at least a bit harder for you, that is a good way to be sure of your dominant type. Your dominant nature will always be opposite of your weakest nature on the Compass.*

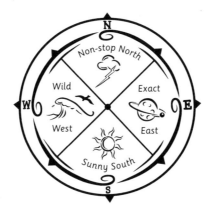

Summary

We can all learn a great deal from the chameleon and other masters of disguise in nature. For instance, in times of special need, many animals change to the color of their surroundings in order to survive. When you use *The Personality Compass* to discover your own nature, and then to strengthen your weaknesses in order to become a more well-rounded and adaptable individual, then people should often think you are the same personality type as they. Being *other-oriented* is the key to effective communication, flourishing relationships and survival in the professional world. This means that you will be able to communicate and network with people according to *their* type, and *their* needs, rather than only according to what is natural and easy for you. You will be able to evaluate quickly what type of person, group or situation you are dealing with, and address them in a way that is based on their nature, not based on your own.

Use the *Compass* to guide you in all of your associations with people, no matter what the circumstances. The principles are the same, and work accurately every time, when you're at home, in the workplace or among strangers. For example, when you find yourself face-to-face with NORTH personality types (no matter what type you are), it is important to look them directly in the eye, stand up straight, and offer a firm handshake, always remembering not to take up too much of their time. When dealing with EAST types (again, regardless of your own direction), it is important to follow proper protocol, be punctual, and relay accurate information, always remembering not to make illogical statements. When conversing with SOUTH types (whether or not you are a dominant SOUTH), it is important to offer a warm smile, a special pat on the shoulder or a hug, and make

296

sincere inquiries as to how they are, and their families, always remembering to take the time to listen to their response. When confronted by WESTS (again, irrespective of your personal nature), it is important to remain loose and relaxed, with a casual, "go with the flow" attitude that encourages spontaneous flexibility, always remembering to maintain a sense of humor and adventure.

Keep in mind that situations, events and jobs also have types of their own. Situations that require strong leadership, or working fast to meet firm deadlines, are NORTH situations that require NORTH skills (no matter what type you are). Those that require careful planning, or detailed analysis, are EAST situations that require EAST skills (again, regardless of your own direction). Events that require keeping people happy, or getting groups to cooperate together as a team, are SOUTH situations that require SOUTH skills (whether or not you are a dominant SOUTH). Jobs that require imagination and creativity, or coordinating numerous different projects or events, are WEST situations that require WEST skills (again, irrespective of your personal nature).

The Personality Compass is a tool to help you recognize what personality type you and others are, and to show you ways to become well-rounded and adaptable. People should have difficulty identifying your true personality type once you have learned and developed the skills needed to move from one direction to another with ease, based on need, rather than on your own personal nature (much like the chameleon). Becoming versatile in the skills of all four personality types does not change your basic nature, but it does broaden your scope and levels of competence, and it improves your ability to get along with people, no matter what type you or they are.

Appendix: North, East, South and West qualities and talents at a glance:

NORTH
Motto: Gets the Job Done Fast

Typical
- Assertive
- Independent
- Decisive
- In control
- Fast-paced
- Self-starting
- Confident
- Authoritative
- Goal-centered
- Ambitious
- Open/direct
- Strong-willed
- Competitive
- Determined
- Hardworking
- Leader
- Task-oriented
- Accountable
- Action-driven
- Courageous

Extreme
- Aggressive
- Pushy
- Controlling
- Sarcastic
- Impatient
- Explosive
- Arrogant
- Argumentative
- Always right/best
- Boastful
- Rude
- Judgmental
- Cutthroat
- Power-hungry
- Domineering,
- Demanding
- Poor listener
- Egocentric
- Insensitive
- Revengeful

Talents
- Getting tasks done fast
- Making quick decisions
- Negotiating terms
- Initiating tasks
- Determining action
- Taking charge
- Competing to win
- Prioritizing importance
- Working hard
- Moving fast
- Setting goals
- Achieving success
- Consolidating steps
- Asserting authority
- Simplifying procedures
- Speeding up processes
- Getting results
- Telling it like it is
- Assessing quickly
- Meeting challenges

EAST

Motto: Does It Right the First Time

Typical
- Quality-centered
- Detailed
- Structured
- Slow-paced
- Deliberate
- Focused
- Methodical
- Organized
- Planner
- Logical
- Analytical
- Proper
- Punctual
- Industrious
- Responsible
- Reliable
- Traditional
- Conservative
- Serious
- Reserved

Extreme
- Perfection-driven
- Humorless
- Inflexible
- Bogged down
- Obsessive
- Oblivious
- Tunnel-visioned
- Habitual
- Critical
- Ritualistic
- Nagging
- Unforgiving
- Unrelenting
- Isolated
- Loner
- Narrowminded
- Tedious
- Critical
- Moody
- Pessimistic

Talents
- Doing things right
- Planning in detail
- Trouble-shooting
- Heading off problems
- Achieving quality
- Analyzing carefully
- Checking for errors
- Organizing everything
- Classifying data
- Following procedures
- Exceeding expectations
- Clarifying exact facts
- Accepting responsibility
- Persuading logically
- Making comparisons
- Measuring precisely
- Doing repetitive tasks
- Keeping records
- Maintaining accuracy
- Showing up on time

SOUTH
Motto: Builds the Best Teams

Typical
- Team player
- Gregarious
- Friendly
- Likable
- Slow-paced
- Laid-back
- Good listener
- Sympathetic
- Peace-loving
- Kind
- Helpful
- Hospitable
- Caring
- Nurturing
- Understanding
- Patient
- Generous
- Giving
- Process-centered
- Easy-going

Extreme
- Dependent
- Shy
- Procrastinator
- Lackadaisical
- Non-assertive
- Meek
- Complainer
- Whiner
- Insecure
- Frightened
- Easily hurt
- Withdrawn
- Martyr
- Vulnerable
- Overzealous to please
- Easily intimidated
- Clinging
- Possessive
- Victimized
- Sad and lonely

Talents
- Building the best teams
- Mediating conflict
- Uniting diverse groups
- Empowering others
- Using diplomacy
- Listening to all sides
- Acting as a liaison officer
- Communicating
- Selling anything
- Putting people at ease
- Offering friendship
- Working cooperatively
- Facilitating processes
- Advising
- Teaching
- Volunteering to help
- Sreading goodwill
- Encouraging peace
- Inspiring loyalty
- Forgiving faults

WEST
Motto: Expands All Horizons

Typical
- Risk taker
- Adventurous
- Fast-paced
- Energetic
- Visionary
- Unconventional
- Innovative
- Creative
- Flexible
- Multi-talented
- Juggles many tasks
- Adaptable
- Spontaneous
- Unstructured
- Enthusiastic
- Sense of humor
- Free-spirited
- Versatile
- Idea-centered
- Dreamer

Extreme
- Practical joker
- Silly
- Error-prone
- Impulsive
- Unfocused
- Scattered
- Unable to finish
- Flighty
- Undisciplined
- Careless
- Disorganized
- Bizarre
- Often late
- Irresponsible
- Frivolous
- Wild and crazy
- Exaggerative
- Inaccurate
- Superficial
- Evasive

Talents
- Seeing possibilities
- Expanding limits
- Solving problems
- Charting a new course
- Coordinating projects
- Motivating people
- Anticipating the future
- Designing creatively
- Taking risks
- Having flexibility
- Juggling various jobs
- Brainstorming ideas
- Delegating tasks
- Visualizing long-range
- Improvising on the spot
- Creating original works
- Loosening up tension
- Inventing new methods
- Adapting to change
- Inspiring innovation

Notes

Chapter One Reviewing the Four Natures of Man

1 C G Jung. *Psychological Types*. New Jersey: Princeton Press. 1971. p 510.

2 W Hardie. *Aristotle's Ethical Theory*. Oxford: Clarendon Press. 1968. p 148.

3 C G Jung. *Psychological Types*. p 516.

4 I Myers and K C Briggs. *A Guide to the Development and Use of the Myers-Briggs Type Indicator*. CA: Consulting Psychologist Press, Inc. 1977. Introduction.

5 I Progoff. *Jung's Psychology and Its Social Meaning*. Garden City, New York: Anchor Press. 1973. p 25.

6 J D Watson and F H C Crick. "*Molecular Structure of Nucleic Acids*" in *Nature*, April 25. 1953. p 737.

7 T Nomi and A Besher. *You Are Your Blood Type*. New York: Pocket Books. 1982. p 25.

8 M Friedman. *Type A Behavior*. New York: Springer-Berlag, 1978.

9 D F Benson (Ed). "Consciousness, Personal Identity, and the Divided Brain" by Roger Sperry in *The Dual Brain*. New York: The Gilford Press. 1985. p 19.

10 R Restek. *The Brain*. New York: Bantam Books. 1984. p 182.

11 R E Ornstein and R F Thompson. *The Amazing Brain*. Boston: Houghton Mifflin. 1984. p 170.

12 T Buzan. *Use Both Sides of Your Brain*. New York: E. P. Dutton. 1974. p 14.

13 E D Abravanel and E King. *Dr Abravanel's Body Type Program for Health, Fitness and Nutrition*. New York: Bantam Books. 1985. pp 33–47.

14 T T Mar. *Face Reading*. New York: Signet Classics. 1974. pp 15–23.

15 A Mendel. *Personality in Handwriting*. New York: Stephen Daye Press. 1947. pp 165–85.

16 W Gallagher. "How We Become What We Are." in *The Atlantic Monthly*, September, 1994. p 42.

Additional references

J Kagan. *Galen's Prophecy*. New York: Basic Books. 1994.

A Toufexis. "What Makes Them Do It." *Time*, January 15 1996.

INDEX